A William H. Jackson construction-era view of D&RG No. 41 on the west slope of Marshall Pass (Museum Collection).

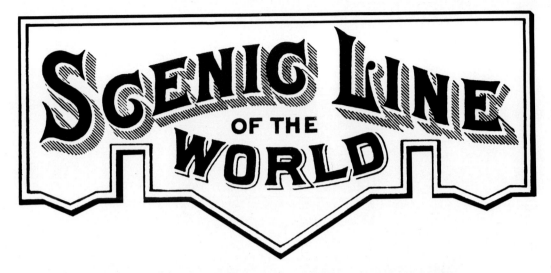

SCENIC LINE OF THE WORLD

by Gordon Chappell

and

Black Canon Revisited

by Cornelius W. Hauck

**the Story of America's Only
Narrow Gauge Transcontinental**

Originally Published in
Colorado Rail Annual 1970
by the

Colorado Railroad Museum

*The two paintings "Rio Grande No. 1" and "Mountain Master"
were created especially for the Rio Grande Railroad Centennial
by Otto Kuhler, distinguished railroad and western artist of Santa
Fe, New Mexico. They are reproduced here through the courtesy
of the Denver & Rio Grande Western Railroad.*

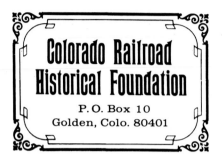

Colorado Railroad Historical Foundation

P. O. Box 10
Golden, Colo. 80401

1977 Edition
Library of Congress Catalog Card No. 70-102682
ISBN 0-918654-33-5

*A sturdy iron horse of the narrow gauge transcontinental (Bald-
win freight hauler No. 273) waits patiently before the Salida
roundhouse one February day in 1908, steam up, ready to do battle with the heavy grades of Marshall Pass. Flanking it are
another D&RG 2-8-0 and the odd slope-back tender from one of
the new "giant" narrow gauge mudhens (2-8-2's) that were then
supplanting the original little iron ponies.*

(Harold K. Vollrath Coll.)

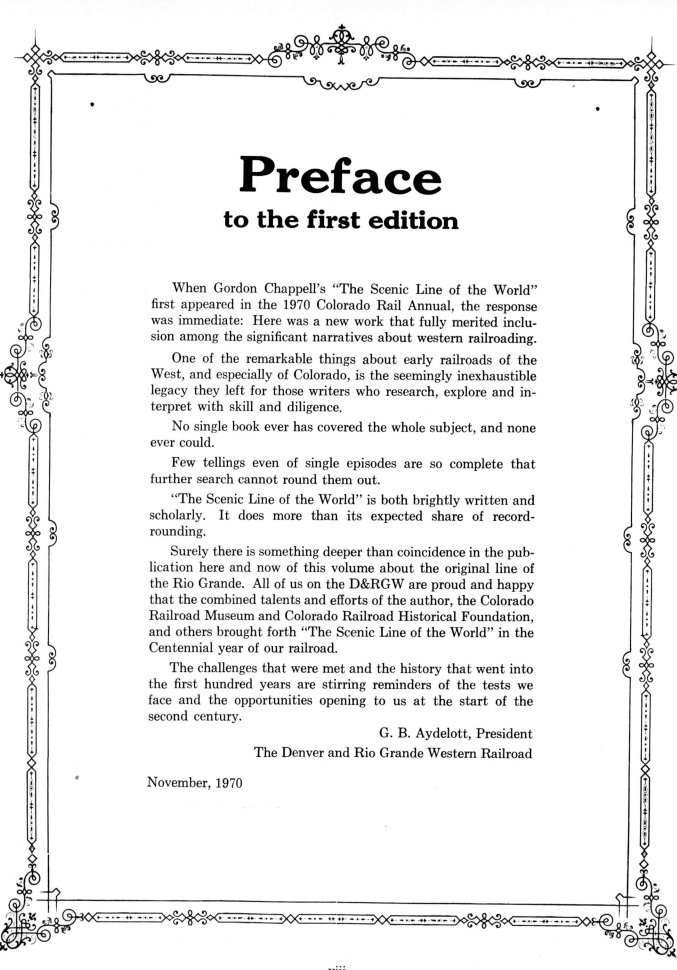

Preface
to the first edition

When Gordon Chappell's "The Scenic Line of the World" first appeared in the 1970 Colorado Rail Annual, the response was immediate: Here was a new work that fully merited inclusion among the significant narratives about western railroading.

One of the remarkable things about early railroads of the West, and especially of Colorado, is the seemingly inexhaustible legacy they left for those writers who research, explore and interpret with skill and diligence.

No single book ever has covered the whole subject, and none ever could.

Few tellings even of single episodes are so complete that further search cannot round them out.

"The Scenic Line of the World" is both brightly written and scholarly. It does more than its expected share of record-rounding.

Surely there is something deeper than coincidence in the publication here and now of this volume about the original line of the Rio Grande. All of us on the D&RGW are proud and happy that the combined talents and efforts of the author, the Colorado Railroad Museum and Colorado Railroad Historical Foundation, and others brought forth "The Scenic Line of the World" in the Centennial year of our railroad.

The challenges that were met and the history that went into the first hundred years are stirring reminders of the tests we face and the opportunities opening to us at the start of the second century.

G. B. Aydelott, President
The Denver and Rio Grande Western Railroad

November, 1970

Going West by Narrow Gauge: A Denver & Rio Grande narrow gauge transcontinental flyer has stopped briefly at the Palmer Lake station, after a 52 mile climb from Denver. While the fireman refills the tender tank (nearly obscured by spray from the fountain) the engineer oils around his Baldwin tenwheeler, and a few passengers take a breath of fresh mountain air. Behind the engine are one of the early flat-roofed express cars, a baggage, two coaches and a Pullman sleeper. In another 719 miles and 32 hours (barring delays) the intrepid tourists will be in Ogden, Utah, and a connection with the Central Pacific to California. (Mellen photo, Kansas State Historical Society Coll.)

Engine crew and friends pose proudly, above, with their shiny Baldwin tenwheeler No. 163, before leaving Denver Union Station with a D&RG passenger train destined for far western points. Its transcontinental route will take it through the spectacular Royal Gorge of the Arkansas — as pictured below, when a group of tourists stopped to view the marvel and have their photograph taken. Tenwheeler No. 167 is followed by a baggage car and five of the Rio Grande's handsome dark red Pullman sleepers, indicating an entirely first-class undertaking. (Both, Museum Collection)

Introduction

Chipeta Falls (Wm. H. Jackson photo)

The Denver & Rio Grande Railway's origins lay in an incredible scheme launched in 1870 by William Jackson Palmer, which envisioned a narrow gauge railroad of miniature proportions linking the new frontier settlement of Denver with the ancient capitol of Mexico City, some two thousand miles to the south. A brave start was made in 1871, when the first 75 miles were completed to Colorado Springs. However, the first trains with their little 12 and 18 ton locomotives and four-wheel cars were hardly more than mechanized pack trains, and the trip to Mexico City promised to be a long one. In fact, as the end of the decade neared, the narrow gauge tracks had not even reached the Colorado border.

Not just inadequate finances had kept the "baby railroad" out of New Mexico; a forceful standard gauge rival in the form of the Atchison, Topeka & Santa Fe had invaded the area, seized one of the three principal projected D&RG routes south — over Raton Pass — and blocked the narrow gauge from expanding into central New Mexico. But the growing flood of commerce to and from the booming mining camps of the Rockies proved an attractive alternative to Mexican dreams, and the D&RG turned west. The La Veta Pass route was redirected towards the San Juan mining regions, while the Arkansas Valley route was pushed north to the fabulous new camp of Leadville. It was the Arkansas Valley line that was to spawn the most ambitious narrow gauge venture of all: from a point 217 miles from Denver, at what is now Salida, a daring rail line was thrown over the Continental Divide at 10,858-foot Marshall Pass, through the Gunnison country and across 567 miles of mountains, canyons and desolate wastelands to Ogden, Utah, and a connection with the famed Central Pacific line to the California coast.

For a half dozen years the Denver & Rio Grande struggled to establish its viability as a narrow gauge transcontinental carrier, only to succumb to the inevitability of standard gauge efficiency. By 1890 the "days of glory" for the narrow gauge transcontinental were over, and the Denver & Rio Grande (along with its Utah counterpart, the Rio Grande Western) had reconstructed the line to standard gauge— and in the process bypassed the spectacular narrow gauge route via Marshall Pass and the Black Canyon of the Gunnison for an entirely new route over Tennessee Pass far to the north.

It is the building and operation (and eventual dismantling) of this unique pioneer narrow gauge transcontinental line that we have documented in text and photo in this book. In Part I we treat the history of the construction and operation of the line across Colorado and Utah during the decade of the eighties. In Part II we review the subsequent history of the narrow gauge remainder in the twentieth century — the scenic and rugged Marshall Pass-Black Canyon route across Western Colorado that gave birth to the railroad's famous advertising slogan, "Scenic Line of the World."

Cornelius W. Hauck

Cincinnati, Ohio
May, 1977

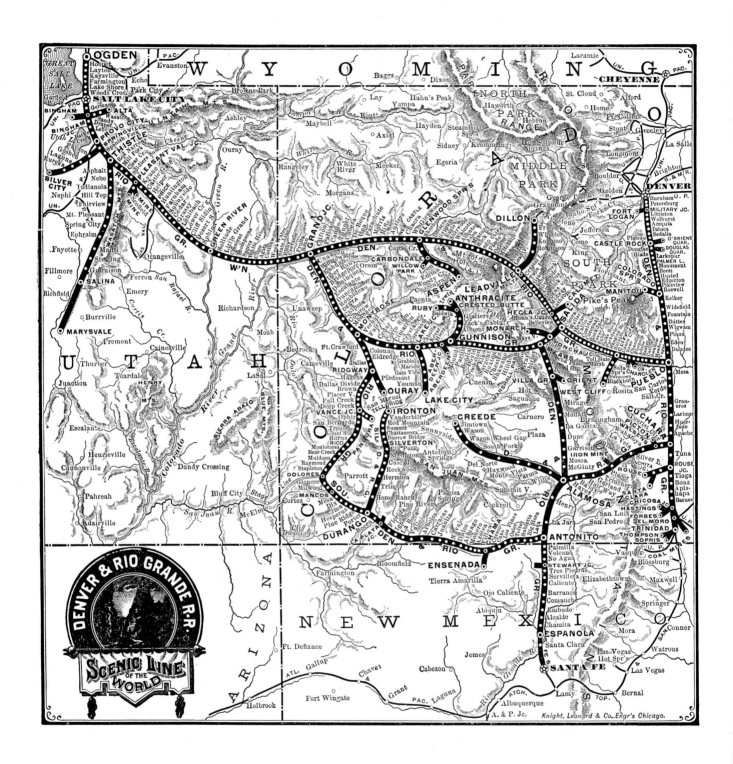

The map above, circa 1895, shows both the original narrow gauge main line via Gunnison and Montrose as well as the succeeding standard gauge Tennessee Pass line via Leadville and Glenwood Springs. Opposite, a colorful cover from a D&RG Tourist's Handbook reflects the flamboyant advertising practices of the Nineties, employed by General Passenger Agent S. K. Hooper to lure crowds of eastern tourists onto the Rio Grande's transcontinental passenger trains. (both, Museum Collection)

The Scenic Route Across the Continent

Crags, Peaks and Parks of the Rockies.

Poole Bros. Chicago

Scenic

909. MARSHALL PASS, WEST SIDE.

Building the line over Marshall Pass in 1881 (Wm. H. Jackson photos from the Colorado College Library Special Collections).

Gauge Transcontinental I:

Line of the World

Gordon Chappell

The 406 on Marshall Pass (Museum Collection).

SCENIC LINE OF THE WORLD! For nearly half of a century the General Passenger and Ticket Agents of the Denver & Rio Grande Railway and its successor companies advertised the scenic wonders of the Colorado mountains which railroad passengers could view from an impressive roster of both narrow and standard gauge trains.

The Denver and Rio Grande Railway was incorporated on October 27, 1870, with William Jackson Palmer, ex-governor Alexander C. Hunt, Dr. William Bell and others among its principal supporters. It was projected as a north-south line connecting Denver with the Mexican border in conjunction with another line (later the Mexican National Railway) from the border to Mexico City. It was to be of a track gauge (width) considerably narrower than the American standard of four feet, eight and one half inches; the Denver & Rio Grande was to have a three foot wide track gauge. It was to be the model for dozens and dozens of other narrow gauge railroads

that were to be built in the 1870's and 1880's, when the nation was in the grip of a "narrow gauge fever" that in some cases reached a point of economic insanity. Following the exhortations of the proponents of the narrow gauge theory, the projectors of the Rio Grande anticipated and realized savings in the costs of locomotives, equipment, rails, ties, and the grading of cuts and fills. The use of narrow gauge permitted the Rio Grande to penetrate the remote mining districts of the mountains of Colorado, New Mexico and Utah much more rapidly and economically than if standard gauge had been used, yet the cost of interchange from standard to narrow gauge and back again at each end of the system would prove a weakness in hauling through traffic and force eventual widening of the railroad's main lines. Nevertheless, a century after its inception, the railroad still profitably operated a narrow gauge passenger train, testifying to the enduring service of the narrow gauge to Colorado trans-

portation, as well as the continuing attraction of Colorado's magnificent mountain scenery.

The early history of the Denver & Rio Grande was plagued with troubles. The first grading of the railway was begun about January 1, 1871. Iron rail weighing 30 pounds to the yard was rolled for the line by the English firm of Barrow Steel in 1870, but was slow to reach Colorado, so that the first spike could not be driven until July 28, 1871. On October 21 the track was completed 75 miles south from Denver to the new town of Colorado Springs, and a passenger excursion rolled over the new rail on October 26 and 27 for the benefit of the Denver press. The initial operator of the road, the construction firm known as the Union Contract Company, turned the railroad over to the Rio Grande company on January 1, 1872, for the beginning of operation of the Denver & Rio Grande Railway.

On southward, construction crews worked their way towards Pueblo,

The original D&RG equipment was very small and quite light in construction, as typified by the petite 4-wheel baggage-mail car shown here in a rare photo taken at the builder's plant. It is no wonder the D&RG was called the "baby" railroad. Although the four-wheel cars soon disappeared, D&RG trains in the seventies continued to be short, light affairs like the one at Manitou (left) powered by little eightwheeler No. 26, the Rio Bravo. Freight was originally handled by moguls like No. 3, the Shou-wa-no, weighing all of 17½ tons. When the D&RG forged west into the mountains, trains grew longer and grades heavier. Eightwheelers for passenger runs were supplemented by new, heavier tenwheelers, like No. 163, pictured at right at Canon City. Coach 80, a Jackson & Sharp product of 1881, was typical of the newer, larger passenger cars purchased for the western extensions. It later became No. 304, underwent substantial rebuilding, and put in many years of service on the narrow gauge. The dainty moguls were soon replaced for freight service by sturdy, low-wheeled 2-8-0's like No. 33, the Silver Cliff (bottom right). The D&RG purchased 53 of these 28-ton Class 56 engines from Baldwin between 1877 and 1880, and even more of the slightly larger Class 60 or C-16 engines; for

years they formed the backbone of D&RG motive power. The advent of the much bigger 2-8-2's resulted in sale or scrapping of the Class 56 engines, but many of the 60 Class (redesignated C-16) remained in service for decades after, and three — the 223, 268 and 278 — are still in existence.

(Two cars, John T. Derr Collection; Manitou and Canon City views, R. H. Kindig-Swain Collection; two locomotives, Museum Collection.)

Successful occupation of the Royal Gorge (the Grand Canon of the Arkansas) proved to be the key to the D&RG's future. The Gorge was so narrow at one point that it was necessary to suspend the tracks over the stream on a bridge-structure, supported from overhead beams. A temporary trestle was utilized in the building of the bridge, as seen below (Denver Public Library Western Coll.). As soon as it was completed, the noted Salt Lake City photographer C. R. Savage journeyed over to record the fact on film, with someone's dog included for a homey touch (right); and dignitaries were guided through the wonder in hastily-equipped flat cars (bottom). (Both photos, Museum Collection). The fame of the new "hanging bridge" spread rapidly.

44 miles from Colorado Springs. Rail for the extension arrived March 20, 1872, and tracklayers reached Pueblo on June 15, the first train service beginning four days later.

This early Denver & Rio Grande was a diminutive railway. The engines were small, seeming almost toys when standing beside contemporary standard gauge power of the Kansas Pacific or Denver Pacific, and the initial freight and passenger equipment was of the four-wheeled type after the English pattern of coaches, "mineral wagons" and "goods vans." But by the end of 1871 the railroad was finished ordering any more of the jewel-like 2-4-0 locomotives such as the *Montezuma*, *Cortez*, and *Ute*, and the trend throughout the decade was towards increasingly heavier 4-4-0, 2-6-0 and 2-8-0 engines which were merely smaller versions of standard gauge Baldwin products. Similarly, the early orders for four-wheeled freight and passenger equipment were not renewed, and eight-wheeled cars, which, like the engines, were merely smaller versions of standard gauge equipment, became typical on the Rio Grande. As time passed the smaller locomotives and cars were increasingly assigned to work train or switching service, and by the end of the decade were seldom seen.

On June 17, 1872, Major General Oliver Otis Howard, United States Army, rode the narrow gauge from Pueblo to Denver, and he later recorded the experience in his memoirs. Head of the Freedmen's Bureau, but on detached duty assigned to negotiate peace with the Apache Indians of Arizona after twelve years of warfare, Howard took several Pima, Pagago and White Mountain Apaches to Washington to meet the Great White Father, President Grant, some months before his celebrated meeting with Cochise of the Chiracahuas. It was the Indians' first experience with a railroad:

I enjoyed the Indians' manifest surprise. Hurriedly leaving the stage they ran to the railway and sat down upon the strange framework. With great curiosity they felt of the cross-ties and fingered the spikes which fastened the iron rails. They looked long and wonderingly at the freight and cattle cars, which were standing near, and then, like children surprised with new gifts, they clapped their hands with glee. A train soon backed down to take us. Our party slowly filed into the small coach to take seats two and two. I was astonished at the evident fear of the Indians. They crouched in abject terror upon the floor between the high backs of the seats and covered their dark faces with their hands.

"What's the matter now, Es-kel-te-ce-la?" Howard asked one of the Apaches through the Hispano interpreter Concepcion.

"We've said we'll go with you. We've given you our whole hearts, and we'll go where you go!" translated the interpreter.

"But what makes them hide their faces and keep so quiet, Concepcion," Howard asked.

"Why sir, they are afraid," Concepcion replied.

But after a few miles of safe and easy riding the Indians' curiosity overcame their fear and they gazed out the coach window in wonder at the settlements they passed and the size and variety of buildings they saw. Before they left Colorado a chief named Miguel told Howard with a sigh that he could not count the mountains any longer, but must rely upon the general to get him back to his homeland.

Another army officer who rode the narrow gauge line in 1872 while en route to his new assignment was Assistant Surgeon R. H. McKay of the Medical Department. A D&RG passenger train was already at the Denver depot when McKay's standard gauge train pulled up beside it.

It was quite a curiosity to me. It looked so very small, I thought of it as a toy affair and wondered if we could make any headway on such a thing. I was surprised and much gratified to soon know how much I had miscalculated its merits. It was a long train and went in and out among the canons and around the mountain sides in an amusing way and with surprising speed. Maybe we would look out and see an engine coming down the track across the canon from us and would discover it to be our own engine puttering along as though pleased with its job.

McKay stayed overnight at Pueblo and the following morning found an army ambulance, that all-purpose army vehicle, to take him over the mountains to Fort Garland.

Unfortunately, the Denver and Rio Grande Railway had been in operation for less than two years when the collapse of Jay Cooke and Company, Bankers, in September, 1873, precipitated the first major depression to follow the Civil War. Progress in construction southward and westward was delayed, for Palmer and his associates had come to depend upon the money markets of the East and Europe for financing. There would develop more or less constant friction with distant stock and bondholders, who were not interested in the railroad strategy of anticipating construction of competing lines with Rio Grande extensions, but wanted only to pocket the rewards of continuing dividends and interest.

Another problem facing the Rio Grande was of its own making; by trying to exploit its own subsidiary townsite companies at the expense of existing towns nearby—a practice employed by Palmer and his associates as long as they controlled the railway—the company incurred the bitter hostility of residents of Colorado, and a lasting legacy of antipathy that would play into the hands of the Rio Grande's competitors. When it did not attempt to exploit its own townsite the railway tried to extort bond issues in support of its construction from settlements that lay ahead. Such policies alienated virtually all of the residents of the strategic town of Canon City, located at the mouth of the Grand Canon of the Arkansas River (now better known as the Royal Gorge).

A third major problem inflicted on the "baby" narrow gauge road was the competition of other (generally standard gauge) railroads, principally in the early years that of the Atchison, Topeka & Santa Fe Railway, whose tracklayers entered Colorado in 1875. There ensued to the end of the decade a race which involved, first, the loss to the Rio Grande of the best route to New Mexico over Raton Pass, and

The "hanging bridge" in the Royal Gorge quickly became a tourist and excursion attraction, particularly as the fight between the Rio Grande and Santa Fe over their rival claims to this narrow portion of the canyon had been well publicized in Colorado. An early seven-car excursion posed for photographer William H. Jackson in the view below. Class 56 Baldwin 2-8-0 No. 32, the "Kit Carson" heads up the westbound train; another unidentified engine is at the rear, pointed east. No doubt the track had not yet been pushed far enough west of the Gorge to reach a wye or turntable, and the second engine would pilot the train back down the canyon to Canon City. Hand-hewn pole ties, 30 lb. rail and square joints are clear indications of raw, unimproved trackwork. (Museum Collection.) Contrast this to the neat stone edging and ballast in the picture at right, taken not long after. The route was already popular for excursions, and as the line was completed through to Salida only one locomotive was needed. (Michael Davis Coll.).

then the bitter contest for the Grand Cañon of the Arkansas. Most of the latter battle was fought out in the courts, clear up to that final arbiter, the United States Supreme Court, whose decision in this case, however, failed to settle the matter. At lower levels, both railroads had judges prejudiced in their favor, the principal nemesis of the Rio Grande road being Judge Moses Hallett in Denver. The "war" did involve some violence; both sides hired gunfighters such as the Santa Fe's William Barclay "Bat" Masterson, and twenty miles west of Canon City the Rio Grande forces constructed rock entrenchments such as "Fort DeRemer" (named after a Rio Grande construction engineer) to prevent the Santa Fe people from building west of the Gorge.

But the Rio Grande's own bond holders, their eyes fixed as if magnetically on interest payments, undermined Palmer's policies and forced him to lease the Denver & Rio Grande to its main competitor. Almost immediately Palmer was charging in court that the Santa Fe had violated the terms of the lease in traffic discrimination designed to hurt Denver and other policies sure to cripple the narrow gauge line; as a matter of fact, Palmer was right. Temporarily the winner with a favorable court decision in his pocket which abrogated the lease, on June 11, 1879, Palmer wasted no time awaiting legal action to oust Santa Fe men from controlling the narrow gauge. Since any delay might result in an appeal verdict in favor of the Santa Fe, he quickly retook his railroad with a company militia armed with rifles and carbines and Colt and Smith & Wesson revolvers. One Rio Grande engineer later recalled how James Massey and a train crew seized the English Fairlie locomotive, No. 101, from the El Moro yard, from under the noses of Santa Fe guards. Hauling a train packed with hired gunmen under Alexander C. Hunt, the Fairlie was raced up the line to Canon City, its men seizing railroad facilities from Santa Fe employees at gunpoint all along the line.

But the courts soon intervened. Palmer sought to cement his accomplishment by placing the road in the

9

This rare photo shows Salida's newly completed Hotel Monte Christo, an ambitious frame structure of interesting architectural style not ordinarily found in the mountain mining camps. Coincidentally the photo shows other interesting features of the yards, such as the little stone depot beyond; an old-style flat roof baggage car at right, bereft of paint; a box at left still lettered "CRS Trust Series B"; a traditional harp switch stand, foreground, is neatly painted white, but the stub switch in front of the depot rates a dwarf target switch stand. The Leadville line runs off to the right, while the new Gunnison Extension veers off behind the Hotel. (State Historical Society of Colo.)

hands of a receiver, but this maneuver failed, and on July 14 another judge dismissed the receiver and two days later forced Palmer and his men to hand the hard-won line back to the Santa Fe people. The court war continued and was resolved only when Jay Gould bought into the Rio Grande, an infusion of capital that enabled the Rio Grande to play the Santa Fe's own game. The Santa Fe had threatened to parallel all existing Rio Grande lines, even commencing a Leadville extension in the spring of 1879; now the Rio Grande threatened to parallel the Sante Fe eastward across the Great Plains, fighting fire with fire. The consequent "Mexican standoff" was concluded by an agreement negotiated in Boston during February, 1880, and known logically as the "Treaty of Boston," although more correctly called the "Tripartite Agreement."

Much to the satisfaction of Rio Grande stockholders, the agreement seemed likely to end the rapid ex-pansion of the Denver & Rio Grande Railway. It prohibited the railroad from building south into New Mexico further than Espanola for a period of ten years, leaving that territory to the Santa Fe Company. Similarly the Santa Fe was prohibited from building into the Colorado mountains — specifically to Canon City and Leadville. The third party to the agreement was the Union Pacific System which, like the Santa Fe, was not to build into the mountains. Thus the Rio Grande, once it reached Leadville, could rest on its laurels and reap fat profits from the traffic in and out of that booming silver camp.

Also entering railroad strategy in the mountains, ex-governor John Evans' Denver, South Park and Pacific Railroad had in October, 1879, negotiated a joint operating agreement with the Denver & Rio Grande concerning its extension from Buena Vista through Chalk Creek Cañon and over Altman Pass—permitting, once that line was completed, D&RG trains to operate into Gunnison. By the spring of 1880, however, Palmer had learned that Jay Gould, who controlled the Union Pacific but had failed to acquire control of the Rio Grande, was as an alternative buying into the South Park road. Palmer began to suspect that the South Park would eventually be absorbed into the Union Pacific System. He was right, and these maneuvers meant that the Union Pacific could circumvent (if not outright violate) the Tripartite Agreement of March, 1880, putting the Union Pacific directly into competition with the Rio Grande in the Colorado mountains. Palmer was determined not to be caught napping again as he had been at the beginning of the contest with the Santa Fe. If the U.P. could violate the Treaty of Boston, so could the D&RG. Palmer would build on to Gunnison in a race with the U.P.-dominated South Park, thus violating also the Joint Operating Agreement with the latter line and earning Evans' antipathy. And

10

Salida was destined to become an important engine terminal on the narrow gauge, particularly after it became the interchange point between the standard gauge and narrow gauge. A photographer climbed up on the roundhouse roof in the 1890's to take these impressive pictures of narrow gauge power at the ready. Identifiable at right are the 409, 267, 401, 274, 404, 268, 218, 62, 213, and 208. In the close-up view below, the 404 has moved onto the table and the 260 has pulled in at the left, while others appear dimly within the shadowy recesses of the roundhouse. Clearly, the D&RG needed plenty of power for Marshall and Poncha, and their biggest and best engines were assigned to the run. (Both photos, Denver Public Library Western Collection.)

the Gunnison Extension would grow into the Uncompahgre Extension, which would continue as the Utah Extension, with another Palmer company building eastward from Salt Lake City to meet it. Thus in a decade the Denver & Rio Grande Railway, which was blocked from building to Mexico City—forever as it developed, instead began construction of an east-west line that would become a major transcontinental link in competition with the original Union Pacific main line located a hundred miles farther north.

Salida: The Founding of a Railroad Town

On March 27, 1880, the "Treaty of Boston" was officially signed and on April 1 a Rio Grande train entered the Royal Gorge, appropriately towed by Engine No. 85, named the *Fort DeRemer*. Even then, complained Chief Engineer James A. McMurtrie, the Santa Fe people dragged out the transfer of their subsidiary Canon City & San Juan Railway's narrow gauge trackage, their "hanging bridge," and other material until April 5, when construction westward could finally resume. True to the Palmerian tradition the railroad builders bypassed the existing Santa Fe sponsored settlement of Cleora to establish a company townsite a few miles farther northwest.

On May 20, 1880, the tracklayers reached the broad valley of the Arkansas north of the Sangre de Cristo Range, where the 160-acre townsite of "South Arkansas" had already been laid out. It was to have streets sixty feet wide, except Walton Avenue which was to be eighty feet, and Railroad Avenue, two hundred feet wide. The first building was erected by C. B. Van Every on Front Street, near the bridge which reached across the Arkansas River to the railroad yards. In the first week Van Every and Fisher, agents of the town company, the railroad's subsidiary, sold $10,000 worth of lots. During the second week they sold another $9,000, and during the third week their sales reached $12,000. By June 5 virtually the whole settlement of Cleora had moved up to the new location, and forty-five business

structures stood on the townsite. That day the *Mountain Mail* published its first weekly issue.

The railroad track-layers, of course, did not pause to watch the town develop; their objective was Leadville. They had laid rail to Nathrop by June 1, 1880, and the first issue of the South Arkansas newspaper reported that track was to be completed to Buena Vista that night, but as usual there were unforseen delays (principally an uncompleted bridge) and the first rail was not actually laid in Buena Vista until about June 9. More important for the future of South Arkansas, the first issue of the *Mountain Mail* on June 5 told its readers that Rowland Cox and a surveying crew that had just finished laying out a rail line west of Colorado Springs through Ute Pass had arrived in South Arkansas for the purpose of beginning a survey for a Denver & Rio Grande extension to the Gunnison country. This meant, of course, that South Arkansas would be the junction of two major rail routes. This would guarantee South Arkansas future growth.

Indeed, South Arkansas was already experiencing a boom. Two passenger trains per day arrived and departed, the shrill whistles of their diminutive engines echoing off the precipitous mountain slopes, the rapid exhausts of their little diamond stacks showering red hot cinders of coal over the unpainted wood and canvas of the town. Every train was loaded with people westbound to "seek their fortunes," some of them remaining in South Arkansas while others went on to Leadville or the Gunnison Country. The best route to the latter was by the Marshall Pass toll road on which Otto Mears had a large force of men working. Travelers who had come eastbound over the road said it would soon be the best mountain road in the country. "Mears means business," concluded the *Mountain Mail*.

Work trains hauling rail and spikes and track bolts and splice bars noisily passed through every day, and by the end of May a large amount of freight destined for Leadville or Saguache or the Gunnison mines came in over the newly laid

rails. Teams were starting out for the Gunnison country every day, as South Arkansas was a natural forwarding point for freight as well as passenger traffic. The firm of Barlow and Sanderson (Southern Overland Mail) meanwhile had taken over a freight car near the depot (which in turn consisted of several other freight cars) to serve as their express and stage office. Stage company stables were under construction near the bridge. The company already had a line running to Leadville, but it wasn't until June 12 that their "Gunnison Short Line" was in operation with eight-passenger coaches. The larger coaches off the Leadville run were to be transferred to the Gunnison route as soon as the railroad reached Leadville. Barlow and Sanderson were continually being put out of business by railroad construction, but while it lasted they made a lucrative enterprise of operating stage lines from the various railheads of the Denver & Rio Grande and the Denver, South Park & Pacific to off-line towns and towns not yet reached by the rails. Their schedule to Gunnison effective June 12 called for the westbound stagecoach to leave South Arkansas at 7 a.m., an hour after the arrival of the morning passenger train from the east, affording the passengers a breakfast and rest stop. The route ran over Marshall Pass with stations at Owens sawmill on Poncha Creek, at the summit, at Sargent's, and at Parlin's. The coaches, some pulled by a four horse hitch, large or more heavily loaded vehicles by a team of six, were supposed to reach Gunnison at 7 p.m. It was a busy little stage line, and the large number of coaches in the Barlow & Sanderson corral gave it the appearance, said the *Mountain Mail*, of a "regular coach manufactory."

The town of South Arkansas still had a rather raw appearance. Many of the buildings were more than half tent, and as early as June 1 the metropolis experienced its first fire when a hot stove pipe ignited the canvas of a structure near the depot. A passerby grabbed a bucket of water and doused the flames before much damage was done. Two men driving teams for the railroad grading crew had been robbed while asleep the previous Sunday night; thus crime accompanied fire as a problem to be faced by the town fathers. There was also a forest fire burning on Poncha Pass to the southwest, which was a source of some concern. Still the town grew. Deputy Sheriff Mix began construction of a two story building at First and E Streets during the second week in June, and on June 10, seven car loads of finished lumber came in by rail for buildings Tom Manless was putting up on First Street. Governor Hunt was also raising a building, this one forty by sixty feet with two stories, located on E between Front and First Streets. Sweet and Company, meanwhile, had taken down the tent they were using for a warehouse near the depot and erected in its place a frame structure. Sparks from the locomotives had burned through the canvas so frequently that the old tent building was beginning to "look like a sieve," said the newspaper, and this was equally true of other such structures near the railroad tracks.

Freight for South Arkansas as well as freight for Saguache, Leadville and the Gunnison country was arriving at such a lively rate that a switch engine had to be assigned to the town. Jim O'Keefe, formerly an engineer on the Union Pacific working between Grand Island and North Platte in Nebraska, was running the little locomotive. The *Mountain Mail* called him a "hard working boy" who "knows how to handle an engine." He also had to handle some eastbound traffic; as early as June 3 freight wagons working for Cummings and Finn brought in three carloads of Leadville bullion for shipment east, and that sort of traffic was rapidly increasing. The passenger trains, meanwhile, commenced service running on time, but as soon as the newspaper bragged about that they began running an hour or two late, much to the editor's annoyance.

F. C. Nims had recently become the General Passenger & Ticket Agent of the railway, and as early as July 31, 1880 the company was reported to be running observation cars on every regular passenger train through the Royal Gorge. One

gentleman recalled going through the Gorge on a train consisting of an engine, baggage car, passenger coach and three sleepers, the *Americano*, the *Aztec* and *El Moro*. "To show us the Royal Gorge, they attached an observation car, which was an ordinary coach sawed off at the seat backs," this New Yorker reminisced. "We almost broke our necks looking up at the cliffs 1,000 feet above, and the genial old conductor stopped the 'observatory' right on the Hanging Bridge." Passengers riding the cars were sure to be liberally sprinkled with cinders from the coal-burning engines of those small trains, so the cars offered liabilities as well as benefits.

West of the Gorge, South Arkansas continued to grow. It had a few female residents by this time, and the first marriage in town took place on Wednesday evening, July 14, when Pearl Fry, daughter of the owner of the Millinery and Fancy Goods store, married A. H. Vernon of Maysville. Whether they took the Denver & Rio Grande out for a honeymoon the newspaper failed to say.

The issue of the *Mountain Mail* for July 24 was the last to be date-lined "South Arkansas," for Governor Hunt had officially renamed the place "Salida," Spanish for "outlet." It was Hunt's intention to give the town a short and appropriate name, and one that was not common elsewhere in the country. Renaming the town was simple enough, but getting the Post Office Department to use the new name was another matter, and mail had to be addressed to "Arkansas, Colorado," for the Post Office had not yet even added the adjective "south."

Within two months of its birth the little town was saucy enough to pick up a gauntlet thrown down by the rival Buena Vista *Times*, which had bragged that the railroad owned a third of their town and asked rhetorically whether South Arkansas could claim as much. The *Mountain Mail* replied that *all* of South Arkansas had been owned by the D&RG, which was rapidly selling its holdings to settlers and businessmen. "You see, Mr. Times," went on the *Mail*,

lots are in demand here and the original owners are not compelled to keep them for want of a chance to sell. We are real sorry if the railroad company can't sell their Buena Vista real estate, because we know they want to awful bad. We don't blame them. In fact we'd be in just the same fix if we were so unfortunate as to be the owners of any of your town lots.

It is interesting to note that other towns such as Conejos, Animas City and Canon City had been as angry as hornets towards the Denver & Rio Grande for playing speculative tricks with company owned townsites to the injury of existing towns nearby. But at least some of South Arkansas' residents were proud that theirs was a railroad sponsored town.

Furthermore, South Arkansas continued to prosper. In fact, the prosperity of the traffic to the Gunnison country resulted in competition for the profits to be had there, for a new toll road was under construction from Maysville over Monarch Pass. The new road first advertised in the Salida newspaper on September 11: "Rates Low." It claimed to be the shortest route by "this low pass" to Gunnison City, Ruby, Gothic, Lake City, Ouray and all points in the San Juan." It would prove effective competition for the somewhat longer Marshall Pass route and give Otto Mears a good reason to sell his road to the railroad.

Other construction crews were working on a telegraph line to connect Salida with Gunnison, Ruby, Crested Butte and Gothic. Wire for the line had reached Salida by the end of July, and for quite a stretch holes had already been dug and poles distributed.

More important for communication and travel to the Gunnison country, Assistant Engineer J. R. DeRemer arrived in Salida in the second week of September and announced that the contract for grading on the Gunnison Extension had been let as far as Maysville and that the contractor would begin work the following week. Sure enough, during the third week of September workmen began driving piles for the railroad bridge across the Arkansas.

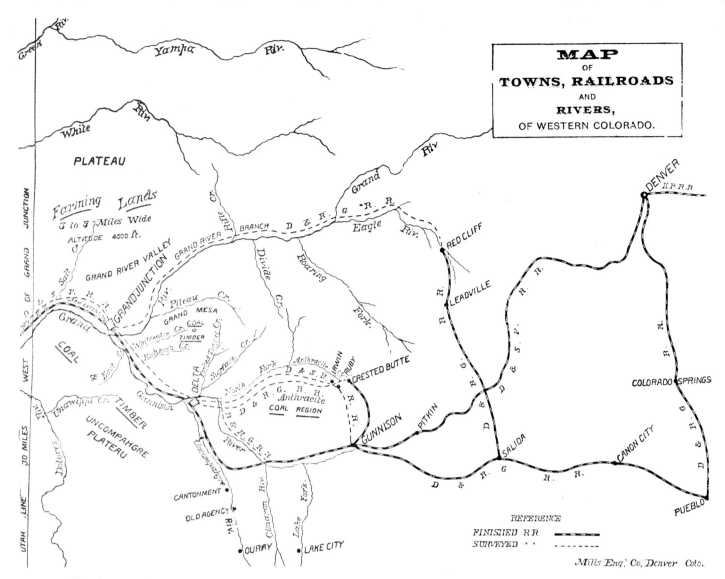

MAP
OF
TOWNS, RAILROADS
AND
RIVERS,
OF WESTERN COLORADO.

REFERENCE
FINISHED R R
SURVEYED " "

Mills Eng; Co, Denver Colo.

This interesting map appeared in the Grand Junction News in October, 1882, and shows not only the Rio Grande and South Park lines then being completed, but a number of projected lines for both roads. (Grand Junction News Coll.)

The Gunnison Extension

By the fall of 1880 it was obvious that Salida was to become an important railroad town. Although the company had already built a board-and-batten depot to replace the box cars used at first, on Monday, August 30, 1880, surveyors began staking out the site of a new stone depot. This impressive little building, 24 by 60 feet in size, went up rapidly; stone work was completed by October 8, and it was finished by the end of the month. Even the window caps and sills were of fancy cut stone, and the editor of the town newspaper commented that the erection of such a structure would indicate that the railroad had "come

to stay" and would inspire confidence among businessmen in the permanence of the town. This was no small matter, for many railroad towns that boomed during construction days disappeared entirely as the railhead moved on. The newspaper added that a "better and more substantial class of buildings" would go up along Salida streets in the future.

Furthermore, on October 2 the railroad officially announced that the company planned to erect a six stall roundhouse in Salida. Obviously Salida's position as the junction of the Gunnison extension with the Leadville-Denver line cemented the town's importance, as the editor of the *Mountain Mail* was well aware.

In Denver, General Manager David Dodge told a Denver *Times* reporter that work on the Gunnison extension would be pushed without any unnecessary delay, and that five hundred men would soon be at work on it. The Denver paper noted that the presence of DSP&P surveying and grading parties working also towards Gunnison would create a "friendly little rivalry" between the two companies as to who could "throw the dirt the fastest." But according to Dodge, work on the Rio Grande line to Gunnison would be "comparatively light"; the South Park line, on the other hand, was faced with the construction of an expensive and troublesome tunnel at the elevation of 11,612 feet. Consequently the Denver & Rio Grande

14

RIO GRANDE EXTENSION COMPANY.

Monthly Estimate for grading Section *2113 (part)*

From Station *O. West of Marshall Pass* to Station *20*

Meyer, McLeod & Co. Contractor.

DESCRIPTION OF WORK.	CUBIC YARDS.	PRICE PER CUBIC YARD.	AMOUNT. Dollars. Cts.	RETAINED PERCENTAGE DEDUCTED. Dollars. Cts.	AMOUNT. Dollars. Cts.	PREVIOUS PAYMENT DEDUCTED. Dollars. Cts.	AMOUNT DUE. Dollars. Cts.
Cleaning and Grubbing,	1 a 50		50				
Earth Excavation,							
Borrowing,							
Wasting Excavation,							
Hard Pan "	333	40	133 20				
Gravel "	272	40	108 80				
Soft Rock "							
Loose Rock "	1149	65	746 85				
Solid Rock "	7229	140	10,120 60				
Haul 100 feet,	2664	2	53 28				
Box Culvert Masonry.							
Arch " "							
Bridge "							
Sustaining Walls,							
Rip Rap,							
TOTALS,			11,213 73				

Amount due this month,

I certify the above to be a true Est

Part - 243 measured by me *Marc...*

W...

C...

RIO GRANDE EXTENSION COMPANY.

Final Estimate for Bridge No. *5 Part*

Station No. *3693*

D & R G Section No. *5*

RAILWAY.

Denigan & Walter Contractor.

Description of Material.	Number of Pieces.	Width & Depth in Inches.	Length in Feet.	Number Feet of Board. Measure.	Cost per Lineal Foot or per 1000.	Amount. Dollars. Cents.
PILING,	117	10 at small end.	18	8146 lft	25d	2115 0
"	1	12x12	12			
BANK SILLS,		10x12	12	168		
CAPS, for Trestles,		10x12	12			
" for Piles,	11	12x12	18	861		
"		12x14	14			
"		10x12				
STRINGERS,	32	7x16	16	4778		
"		7x16				
BRIDGE TIES,	118	6x8	10	1920		
BRACES,		3x9				
"						
POSTS,		10x10				
"		10x10				
"		10x10				
SILLS,		10x12				
"		10x12				
GIRTS,	8	6x8	16	512		
GUARD TIMBERS,	8	6x6	16	512		
2 in. PLANK, for Culvert Sides,		14 inches wide.				
2 in. " " "		16 " "				
3 in. " " "		14 " "		8754 ft	750	65 65
3 in. " " "		16 " "				
PLANK,		2 inches.				
" Earth Exc 50 cu yds		3 "		11	25d	1
						278 15
TOTAL,				*Sur Payt*		350 30

Amount due this *Ninth* $27.81

I certify the above to be a true estimate of the amount of work done on bridge No. 5

Section No. *29 it* Station No. *3693* measured by me *March 31* 188*7*

Assistant Engineer.

R L Eagle Asst Engineer.

The construction of the D&RG was a major undertaking involving the coordination of many different contractors and labor forces, often simultaneously at different points on the line. To systematize supervision and maintain some control over costs and construction fund requirements, the Rio Grande Extension Company utilized standard detail estimate forms such as these. (Rio Grande Coll., State Historical Society of Colo.)

had a big advantage over the South Park and expected to beat that line into Gunnison. The people living in the Gunnison country, however, less well informed than the D&RG management, long held to the belief that the South Park line would lay track into Gunnison many months before the Rio Grande.

Beyond Gunnison, Dodge was pretty vague as to Rio Grande intentions. He said it would depend altogether on what points held out the best inducements for business and were most easily reached. The railroad was apparently up to its old tricks, trying to stimulate settlements ahead of the railhead to compete with each other to see which could offer the railroad the best deal. Unfortunately for the D&RG, beyond Gunnison there were just not many towns in existence, so playing coy this time availed the Denver & Rio Grande nothing.

By October 2, 1880, men and teams were at work on the grade between Salida and Poncha Springs, but it was still not known locally whether the railroad intended to cross Marshall Pass or Monarch Pass. The *Mountain Mail* correctly guessed that the line up to Maysville on Monarch Pass would prove to be merely a branch. In fact, the D&RG was carrying on negotiations through construction manager Robert F. Weitbrec which culminated in the sale of the Marshall Pass Toll Road to the railway company for $13,000.

There was also talk of a Rio Grande branch line over Poncha Pass to Saguache and another up the Ute Trail and across the South Park. Meanwhile wagon and coach traffic to and from the Gunnison country was about equally divided between the Monarch and Marshall toll roads, and it was "right lively."

In Salida on October 16, D&RG Agent Frank Crozier announced that track on the Gunnison Branch would be laid to the little village of Poncha Springs within three weeks, and that a supply station would then be established at the springs— the railhead in other words. (American railroads having developed many of their practices from examples set by the military establish-ment, which was only logical since many railroad executives like Colonel Palmer had been soldiers. The common term used by D&RG employees for the end of track on a construction project was "the front." Poncha Springs would thus, for a period, become "the front.")

By October the railroad management had also decided to put up machine shops in Salida, and by the end of that month work on the excavations and foundations for the roundhouse was progressing rapidly.

The first rail to be laid on the Gunnison Extension was spiked into place on Thursday, October 21, 1880. The bridge over the Arkansas River in Salida had just been completed, and tracklaying rapidly progressed westward on the completed grade. The grading crew were by that time working above Poncha Springs, and it was there that the Gunnison Extension experienced its first casualty. Some unknown grievance caused a grading boss to beat up one of his men; then later, still nursing a grievance, he picked up a carving knife from the cook room and told the laborer that he would cut his heart out. The latter pulled a revolver and shot the boss in the neck, killing him instantly. The killer surrendered to the authorities and was acquitted by Justice Pinckney of Maysville on the basis of self defense.

The line also experienced its first derailment that month, at 6 p.m. on October 27. As a freight train was backing in on the Gunnison Branch the caboose jumped the track and ran into the depot platform, chewing some of the planks into kindling. A collision between two freight trains in the Arkansas Canon near Texas Creek the previous Saturday night had added to the Rio Grande's misfortunes. Another wreck occurred right in Salida on November 9 when a locomotive jumped the track and ran into Mack's warehouse, damaging the building and "demolishing doors and windows by the wholesale."

Speaking of locomotives, as a consequence of its rapid expansion, the railroad placed with Baldwin Locomotive Works (Burnham, Parry, Williams & Company) the largest single order for engines that had been made up to that date. And it would remain the largest narrow gauge locomotive order ever made. On October 27, 1880, it contracted for another thirty-two locomotives, making a total of 124 purchased since November 1, 1879, 92 of which had been delivered. The Baldwin works at Philadelphia was hardly able to keep up with the demand.

On November 14, 1880, track on the Gunnison Extension was completed to Poncha Springs, where the line was to fork with a seven mile branch to Maysville on Monarch Pass, while the main line turned south to climb Poncha Creek Canon towards Marshall Pass. An additional week of grading and the laying of side tracks was necessary before the shipping terminus could be moved from Salida to Poncha Springs; the line was officially opened for scheduled traffic on Monday, November 22, with connecting Sanderson stages to points west over Marshall Pass.

Grading crews continued to work between Poncha Springs and Owen's saw mill six miles up the canon. Here the Santa Fe had done some advance grading during the railroad war of the late '70's on a line heading apparently for the San Luis Valley, and some of their grade was incorporated into the Rio Grande line, saving much work. But by the morning of Thursday, November 18, the temperature in Salida had dropped to 23 degrees below zero, and a number of laborers had quit because of the severity of the weather. Again, as a coincidence in timing, the railroad was building an extension over a major mountain pass in the dead of winter, and it was an unpleasant job indeed.

In Salida, the pay car rolled in to do some business. Across the tracks the roundhouse was rapidly going up, and the platform at the depot was extended to cover all the ground between the depot and the tracks on either side. With money in their pockets the railroad employees headed for the booze halls and the red light district. Two of the graders got into a quarrel one evening in Deverux's saloon and one of them hit the other on the forehead with a revolver, making an ugly gash. By the following week the Salida "cala-

16

boose" was ready for participants in any further affrays.

The *Mountain Mail* for December 4 reported that graders were "making the dirt fly" along the line up Poncha Creek despite cold weather, and three coaches full of laborers for the Gunnison Extension had gone up the line to Poncha Springs. Travelers over Poncha Pass reported a two foot snow fall at the summit.

Over on the western slope, a Denver & Rio Grande surveying crew, consisting of sixteen men, worked its way into Gunnison City on January 8, 1881, and camped at the corral ground below the old recorder's office. J. H. Morton, head of this particular crew, announced that they were surveying a route towards Salt Lake City by way of the Cimarron, and expected eventually to meet a party under Fred Mathyas working eastward from Salt Lake. It was the first indication to citizens of Gunnison that they would be on a transcontinental main line of railroad. There was at least one benefit to carrying out such survey work in winter; at this time of year most of the streams would be frozen over and the surveyors could literally walk on water—a major advantage in running surveys through a precipitous gorge such as the Black Canon of the Gunnison.

During the first week in February, D&RG crews commenced tracklaying on the branch line from Poncha Springs to Maysville, seven miles up the Monarch Pass road. Fifty-six men and twelve teams were at work on the branch line, and the track layers following the graders reached the vicinity of Maysville during the last week of February. As usual it took time to put in switches and side tracks, and the railroad was having an argument over some obscure matter with the Maysville town council, so although the track was serviceable by March 15, traffic did not begin to use the line immediately. The first car load of freight was not received in Maysville until Monday, March 21, and the first regular passenger service there ran on Sunday, March 29. The D&RG had already erected a depot there and by March 26 the telegraph line to Maysville was in service.

Meanwhile, tracklaying also proceeded on the line up Poncha Creek. By the middle of February more than 1,100 men and 150 teams were at work on the Gunnison Extension, laying rail and ties on the frozen ground. The railroad company negotiated with Mr. Owens for land on which to build a depot near his sawmill. Owens was to retain ownership of the townsite, if a town should grow there. The place was renamed "Mears," after the Indian commissioner who had built the toll road on which some of the Marshall Pass rail line would be laid. (A year or two later a station between Poncha Springs and Mears was named "Otto," so that subsequently the westbound passenger saw station signs that read in sequence, "Otto" and "Mears.")

Business in Salida had diminished somewhat once the "front" had been moved up to Poncha Springs, and then to Mears, but there was enough to require an addition to the stone depot. It was rumored that Salida would become a division point on the railroad, with all the shop facilities and offices that would entail. A railroad hospital would also become a necessity, and another ten stalls to the roundhouse, making it a sixteen stall roundhouse.

Out on the Gunnison Extension, meanwhile, railroad officials debated whether to make Mears or Silver Creek, further up the valley, the next forwarding point for passenger and freight traffic after Poncha Springs. The two were close together (2.2 miles) and the grading beyond Mears to Silver Creek was easy. The rails were spiked down at Mears on March 26, and on the following day Mears was made a temporary terminus for freight and passenger traffic until April 1, when Silver Creek became the terminus.

"Large gangs of men are now employed on the Gunnison extension of the D&RG road and the dirt and rock are being thrown lively," reported the Gunnison *Review* on April 2:

An immense amount of work has been done on both sides of the range, and a large amount will yet have to be done even before the iron horse will be able to snort on the summit, 10,500 feet above tide.

The newspaper told its readers that the railroad crossed the stage road three times between Poncha and the summit, and that at the summit grading crews were excavating a long cut fifty feet deep through the ridge south of Mount Ouray, thus avoiding the necessity of tunneling. The view, said the paper, was one of the grandest in the state. That down the Tumitchi (now Tomichi) Valley was excelled only by the rugged scenery of the Royal Gorge. At the summit grading crews had to work amid snowbanks two to four feet deep. The snow on the east slope of the range required passengers to transfer from stagecoach to sleigh, and "with ten passengers packed like sardines it is anything but a pleasure trip crossing the back-bone of the continent."

The west slopes, however, were almost bare, and the mud "almost unfathomable for pedestrians," said the *Review*. Down in the Tumitchi Creek valley a Rio Grande work force had been digging ditches to change the course of the creek in order to permit the railroad as straight a course as possible. Stagecoach passengers who endured this quagmire found welcome accommodations at Joseph Sargent's ranch, which had been pressed into service as a stage stop on the Sanderson line. Passengers could stay there overnight and be fed supper and breakfast. Those who managed to get over Marshall Pass at all that spring were lucky; some unfortunate souls who chanced to travel by stage when the toll road was completely closed by snow, slides, or mud had to endure a trip to Gunnison all the way by Saguache and Cochetopa Pass, circling far to the south. The *Review* in April of 1881 reported frequent land slides on the west slope of the pass due to rapid thawing, and insisted that there was not a "worse road in the State" for freighting at that time. "It is utterly impossible for a wagon loaded with freight to successfully make the trip with the road in its present condition," said the newspaper. "Freight is piled up by the roadside in many places and it will be some time yet before it can be hauled through." Even for stages the road was a tricky proposition. One near-

A hardy track gang is busy throwing
some dirt and rock "ballast" on the new,
raw track well up on the east side of
Marshall Pass, while a construction train
negotiates the horse-shoe curve below.
In accepted construction-period practice
near the "front," the train has an engine
headed up hill at one end and another
pointed down hill at the other. (Above,
Wm. H. Jackson view from Univ. of Wy-
oming Coll.) At right, a similar construction train is in the siding at Gray's, 19
miles out from Salida and only 6 miles
from the top of Marshall Pass. The near
engine is no. 401, while the far engine
is unidentified. Construction camp cars
occupy the siding on the left, and the
ground is littered with various construction debris. (Museum Collection.)

ly turned over, balancing on two wheels while passengers wedged so tightly inside that they could hardly move held their breaths and a passenger riding on the box with the driver jumped to save himself. The Marshall Pass toll road was hardly pleasant, and the railroad which now owned it had little interest in keeping it in any better condition than was necessary to permit the equipment of grading contractors to use it.

Silver Creek was of course a booming construction camp. By the middle of April it had fourteen large business tents, "eight of them saloons and dance halls," according to the Gunnison *Review*. Tracklaying had ceased at that point until the grade to the summit was completed, for progress was slowed by a chronic shortage of rail. Quite a number of bidders had obtained grading contracts for the line: Myer, McLeod & Company; Coby and Rankin; Clark Lipe & Company; Kenner, Coolridge & Company; Florida Forbes & Company; Carrico & Fay; J. J. Cummings & Company, and others. Some of these even subcontracted portions of their work; thus McCaffrey & Company obtained work from Myer, McLeod; and Pat Fay did some work on the Clark Lipe & Company contract. J. R. DeRemer was the engineer for much of the project, and he had a sizeable staff of assistant engineers to keep an eye on the grading contractors. These included Rowland Cox, Charles Boyd, F. Meredith Jones, Fred Mathyas, Otto Reizler, Harry King and many more. Green and Fordy had the contract for laying steel. Grading crews lived in tent camps near their work, while the rail laying gangs lived in a boarding train parked near the end of track.

Labor was one of the major problems. At the same time the railroad was building the Gunnison Extension, it was also building the San Juan Extension over Cumbres Pass towards Durango; the Albuquerque Extension, on which construction had ceased at Espanola on December 31; the Eagle River Extension over Ten Mile (Fremont) Pass north of Leadville; the Grape Creek Extension to Westcliff; and the South Park extension through Platte

Snowsheds were built as rapidly as the line was pushed forward. Above, a new shed protects a curve under the shadow of Mt. Ouray; the construction outfit cars sit on an unfinished siding alongside. (Bancroft Library, Univ. of Calif. Coll.) Engine 54, the "Ruby Camp", poses amidst the timbers of the unfinished shed on Marshall. (Denver Public Library Western Coll.)

19

The line over Marshall Pass ascended a range of mountains both forbidding and overwhelmingly beautiful. These views taken by Jackson from the Poncha Pass area, southwest of Salida, show the eastern approach to Marshall unusually well. In the panoramic view above, looking north from the flank of Poncha Pass and across the Marshall Pass line in the valley, 14,229-foot Mt. Shavano dominates the horizon, with the Collegiate Range beyond. Above right, the Marshall Pass line can be seen starting in the valley (foreground) and zigzagging up the flank of Mt. Ouray, the massive peak in the background. The upper portion of this same view of Mt. Ouray can be seen, bottom right, looking west from the wye at the top of Poncha Pass. The same little one-car Jackson photographic train can be seen in each photograph. (All, Wm. H. Jackson photos, State Historical Society of Colo.)

20

MT. OURAY FROM PONCHA PASS.   PHOTOGRAPHIC CO.

Canon; and the competing South Park company was building Alpine Tunnel and grading towards Gunnison. This created an overwhelming demand for labor, and since November 1879 the railroad had been shipping an average of at least a thousand laborers per month from Denver and Pueblo to the many grading camps in the Rockies. In addition the company had advanced the fares of 200 men from Canada, many of them French Canadian lumberjacks hired as tie cutters, 250 from St. Louis, 300 from Chicago, and 1,000 from points in Kansas. These laborers all agreed to refund the cost of their transportation once they had earned it working for the railroad. Fat chance of that! "In nearly all cases the men deserted," Construction Manager Weitbrec reported on March 16, 1881; "Many went to the mines, a few returned to their homes, and the Lord probably knows where the rest are."

Total expenditures for recruiting this labor were $41,350, of which only $8,000 in fares had been recovered; in other words there was a dead loss of $33,350 in attempting to find workers. As a result Weitbrec concluded that unless a man could raise enough money to pay his own railroad fare and expenses, he wasn't the sort the railroad should hire anyway. Even Weitbrec's attempts to recruit Negroes from the South met with little success. The search extended as far as Italy. Railroad building was a difficult and costly business, and finding enough labor was not the least of a construction manager's worries.

Another problem according to the Gunnison *Review* was a shortage of rail. However by May 7, 2,500 tons of European steel was en route by barge on the Mississippi from New Orleans to St. Louis, and another 3,000 tons was awaiting barge shipment.

Stage traffic was now so heavy that many people had to lay over at Silver Creek for a day or more. The Gunnison *Democrat* of May 4 claimed that the Sanderson stages could not carry half the people who wanted to get to Gunnison. The Gunnison *News* noted that the railroad was making its presence felt: "Railroad men are in our midst; our

grocers are making out bills of provisions for the railroad camps near by; our hardware men are furnishing supplies of nails, tools, &c.; our lumber merchants are called upon for lumber with which to build the railroad men houses and sheds." These were of course the first of the grading crews working through Gunnison, for the "front" or end of track was still at Silver Creek. Nevertheless it was reassuring to know that by the middle of April the graders had passed on and were already two miles below the town.

The stage trip into Gunnison from Silver Creek was about 53 miles, with the stage making the overnight stop at Sargent's and arriving in Gunnison at 4 p.m. the following afternoon. By April 16, J. L. Sanderson himself had arrived in the Gunnison country in order to stock stage stations on a new line between Gunnison, Ruby and Gothic via Crested Butte. He expected to have stages running on this route about May 1, using a four-horse Concord coach.

Silver Creek was making the most of its brief existence as a construction camp. The usual class of citizens was present to prey on the railroad builders' wages. "Silver Creek has had more bunko men than could prosper, and they are leaving for other camps," claimed the Salida *Mountain Mail*. By May 21 according to the Gunnison *Review* the town had 75 buildings "of all sorts." Among them were four forwarding (freighting) and commission houses, five groceries, two clothing stores, two hotels, one drug store, three bakeries, two meat markets, two blacksmith shops, one wholesale liquor store, two butter and egg depots, and "restaurants and saloons without number." The railroad opened an express office on May 11, with J. G. Knight, formerly the agent at Poncha Springs, in charge.

By May 21 the grade was completed seven miles west of Silver Creek, the grading contractors had arrived, expecting to begin laying track very soon. The big rock cut at the summit proved troublesome and excavation work went slowly, but down to the west the grade was rapidly nearing completion and three grading camps were now lo-

cated between Sargent's and Parlin's Ranch.

Salida at this time was as busy as ever, although the newspaper was still fuming about the inability of various people to get the new name of the town straight. Most infuriating, the railroad itself persisted in calling the place "South Arkansas" in its timetables. Then when in May it finally did change the name, it merely emulated the Post Office Department by calling it "Arkansas." "When will we get this thing straightened?" inquired the newspaper editor.

To stock this and other new extensions, locomotives began arriving at Denver from the Baldwin plant in Philadelphia. Numbers 400 and 401, named respectively the "Green River" and the "Grand River" rolled in on flatcars early in May. Two more, the "Shoshone," Number 402, and the "Roaring Fork," Number 403, arrived on May 13, and four additional locomotives were expected to arrived daily until the contract was fulfilled. Freight and passenger cars were likewise arriving daily in Denver by standard gauge, and there was material stored in the shops for 2,000 additional freight cars. Eight Pullmans were expected in June, and as early as April the company had ordered refrigerator cars that were capable of being lifted bodily from standard to narrow gauge trucks, in order to go straight through to points west of Denver in narrow gauge territory.

By May 28, Green & Foody had commenced laying rail west from Silver Creek, and even towns far from the projected railway were feeling its influence. A newspaper in the remote mining camp of White Pine carried an advertisement for a "D&RG Saloon." But residents of Gunnison now had two railroads to watch. Not only the Rio Grande company but the Denver, South Park and Pacific had grading crews in the area. Although Alpine Tunnel on Altman Pass was not holed through, the tunnel builders reportedly had only 630 feet to go and expected to tunnel 220 feet per month. East of the tunnel, tracklayers on that line had reached St. Elmo by April 30, and grading crews were already at work between

Pitkin and Gunnison southwest of the tunnel. As both railroads raced for the river above the Black Canon, the Gunnison *News* speculated that a railroad war in the canon of the Gunnison might be in the making. But all of this was premature, and Alpine Tunnel still held some nasty surprises for the South Park's builders.

D&RG men, too, were increasingly active in the Gunnison country. A survey crew during the first week in May went out to run a second survey for a line north to Crested Butte, where in April the railroad had purchased extensive coal interests owned by Howard Smith and George Holt. The Denver *Tribune* called it the best coking coal that had been found in the state. Given this prospective traffic and its importance as a source of fuel for engines, some of the grading crews west of Gunnison were pulled off their jobs there and put to work grading a branch line to the Crested Butte mines.

Tracklaying still moved westward at a snail's pace on the eastern slope. Aligning the rail to the proper gauge on almost continuous curves and grades was no easy task. By June 4 the crews of Green & Foody were spiking down track ten miles west of Silver Creek. Several train loads of "iron" rolled up to the "front" every day. Right to the end Silver Creek kept its character as a rough construction camp; on June 16 the camp had a "regular old fashioned round-up," according to the Salida newspaper; "a big crowd of the boys went on a spree and had a high old time." One man was shot in the leg, though not seriously.

The following day the Salida paper was reporting the arrival of the Duke of Sutherland and his "swell party of blarsted Britishers," properly chaperoned by officials of the railroad. It was Sutherland who had sold the Rio Grande the English Fairlie locomotive. After a breakfast at Gray's Hotel in Salida on June 17, they had gone up the line, probably to Leadville, although they may have visited the end of track on Marshall Pass as well.

The Salida newspaper also carried the usual reports of railroad misfortunes. A train on the canon line east of Salida ran over three deer a few miles below town, fortunately without derailing.. "The engine will probably be taken up for killing game out of season," jested the *Mountain Mail*. A more serious accident occurred a week later when the engine of an early morning westbound freight, starting into a side track to allow a passenger train coming up behind to pass, jumped the frog and turned over, taking several cars off the track with it. No one was injured, but passenger trains in all directions were delayed for several hours and Gray's Hotel in Salida had a record crowd wanting breakfast.

West of the Great Divide

At seven p.m. on June 21, 1881, the westbound Barlow and Sanderson stagecoach pulled into Gunnison. As the weary passengers stepped down, they announced that at 9:30 that morning theirs had been the first passenger train to arrive at the summit of Marshall Pass. They reported that the stretch just opened from Silver Creek to the summit was "grand in scenery" and, somewhat to their surprise, "smooth and easy to ride upon." The Gunnison *News-Democrat*, the two papers having merged, was positively elated:

And this is not the best of the news. It is positively stated by those in authority that the terminus of the Gunnison branch will be at "Sargents" by the Fourth of July. From Sargents to Gunnison as everybody knows is a comparatively level county, and as the larger part of the road from that point to this has been already graded, there is little doubt but that the whistle of the first locomotive ever heard in this valley will serenade the people of Gunnison by the first of August.

Needless to say, this schedule was overly optimistic and was not met. The Fourth of July did not see the railroad reach Sargents, but it was the occasion for a special excursion from Salida to the summit, the first such excursion on the Gunnison line.

At 6:20 a.m. on the holiday a party of twenty-five, a quarter of them children, took the morning train out of Salida for the summit of the main range. At Silver Creek, now renamed Shirley, the train was turned on the wye and backed up the pass. Many excursionists stood on the end platform of the first car as it was pushed "up the steep grade, around the mountain sides, over deep gorges and through dense forests . . ." At the summit the excursionists had a snow-ball fight, and before long were so chilled they had to build a fire. A brief shower came down off the slopes of Mount Ouray and drenched the party, and they retired to the coaches. Shortly thereafter the train was taken four or five miles down the "windings, twistings and curvings of the road as it hunts for low land" on the west side of the pass. The party finally returned to Salida in an afternoon storm which, according to the *Mountain Mail*, didn't hurt them, "as they sometimes use water." It had been a pleasant trip and the passengers all thanked Conductor Abbott for a good time.

A less happy incident was recorded by the *Mountain Mail* two days later. On July 6 the Gunnison Extension recorded its first rail fatality when a train ran over a man near Poncha Springs. The body was so badly mangled that no one could tell who the unfortunate victim was.

By this time the town of Gunnison had become quite excited over the question of location of the D&RG depot. The original townsite of Gunnison had been laid out in the spring of 1879 (although prospectors had visited the area as early as 1861 and a few had settled there). During the winter of 1879-80, however, the town company split and the dissident faction made a deal with the Denver, South Park & Pacific, pooling about 1,000 acres to form a new townsite known as West Gunnison — which was sometimes called the "Mullin Patch" in honor of one of its principal organizers, hotel owner Loudon Mullin. By the middle of March, 1881, the rival settlements of new and old (or west and east) Gunnison were competing for the terminus of the Rio Grande road, and it appeared that the D&RG, like the DSP&P, had decided to build its station and facilities in West Gunnison. "Of course this makes the old town kick," com-

Eleven miles west of Salida was Mears Junction; here the "Villa Grove Branch" turned south across low Poncha Pass into the San Luis Valley. The line branched off the Marshall Pass line on the north, curved around on a great loop over the main line, and then worked its way back along the side of the hill above Mears before turning south. In the view above, taken just west of the junction, a D&RG work train is descending towards Mears during construction days. The engine is one of the little 56 or 60 class 2-8-0s, probably no. 83. More outfit cars are set out on the siding at extreme left. At left, a mixed train (six box, a baggage and a coach) is posed climbing up the hill behind the Mears depot, where the track looped south towards Poncha Pass. This line was later extended to Alamosa, and through passenger service to the San Juan country took this route during the 1890s when the Veta Pass line was closed for standard gauging. (Both, State Historical Society of Colo.)

mented the editor of the *Elk Mountain Bonanza*, who was wryly watching the contest from the town of Gothic located to the north;

> and as it possesses men capable of understanding the manipulation of railroads, it cooly hooks its thumbs in its suspenders and tells the railroad that it cannot run through its corporation. Moreover it goes out, takes in plots and surveys additions; extends from the bluffs on the south to the hills on the north, and makes Gunnison take in the whole width of the valley.

Now, thought the residents of "old" Gunnison, the railroad would have to agree to give their town a passenger depot too; but the old town was willing to settle for nothing less than the whole works, freight depot, machine shop and roundhouse included. The *Bonanza* wished the "old town" boys luck: "staunch Kubler," "scheming Mac, the lawyer," and Sammy Gill, the "moneyed power"; things must "go *their way* or 'bust'." But the railroad apparently found a legal way around the sharpsters of Gunnison City, for by the end of April the depot had been firmly located at the foot of 14th Street in the "new" Gunnison. "How do the Mullin patch and Gunnison senior people compare notes now?" inquired the *Bonanza*. By this time the D&RG, like the South Park road, was one-third owner of the West Gunnison Town & Land Company, so the Rio Grande was trying to make money from land sales again; but the prospective arrival of a second railroad in the Gunnison country did not permit Palmer's men the freedom in establishing a competitive townsite they had enjoyed in the past. Thus they had to settle for part interest in West Gunnison, which was so close to the established town of Gunnison that the newer townsite never succeeded in killing off the old. The settlement of the depot site also killed off the lively sport of trying to guess the location; "Side bets have been frequent that it would be here, then there, and over yonder," commented the Gunnison *Review* on April 30.

There was also trouble with the South Park line over its route through "old" Gunnison, South Park engineers wanting to use Tumitchi Avenue, one of the main streets. The Gunnison City Council thought it had worked out an agreement by which the railroad would use San Juan Avenue and at its meeting on June 2 granted right-of-way down that street. But on July 6, South Park surveyors ran a line of stakes down Tumitchi Avenue. Mayor Kubler sent Marshal Bailey out to follow the surveyors and pull up all the stakes. He told them if they repeated the offense they would be arrested and jailed. Gunnison was not satisfied having an argument with *one* railroad; it wanted to argue with *two*.

West of Gunnison heavy work on the grade had been going on since March and by the latter part of April Gunnison residents could hear heavy blasting at frequent intervals two miles west of the town. On Saturday evening, April 23, the D&RG grading contractors set off one blast that shook every building in the city. "It was the most terrific explosion we have ever heard in Colorado," commented the editor of the Gunnison *Review*. The grading, of course, was the most difficult task in building a railway. The building of bridges, trestles and culverts followed, and W. F. McIntyre of Gunnison had the contract for such structures through the town.

On the afternoon of July 16, 1881, regular passenger train service reached Sargents for the first time, and that ranch became the next construction camp. The railhead was now only thirty-two miles from Gunnison. The stagecoach, which had left the new terminus at one p.m., had not arrived until 7:30 as a consequence of the train being late. It was necessary for trains to run very slowly over the new track for several days until it settled and the gauge was adjusted.

Nevertheless regular freight service from Sargents was begun July 18. "There are probably fifty firms now doing business there, the most of whom are occupying tents," reported the Gunnison *Review*. McIntire, Bean & Duval, James McGee, W. D. Ainslie, J. J. Harris, and McGavock & Tate were all operating

In its climb over Marshall Pass, the D&RG line worked back and forth along the flanks of the mountains, zigzagging in and out of side valleys and around spurs to gain altitude. In 25 miles the line went from near 7,000 feet at Salida to 10,858 feet at Marshall Pass — an average grade of over 3½% for the entire distance beyond Poncha Springs. The west approach from Sargents was equally steep. The meanderings of the line are well shown in this old engraving used by the D&RG to publicize the "marvelous engineering" embodied in the line. (Museum Collection.)

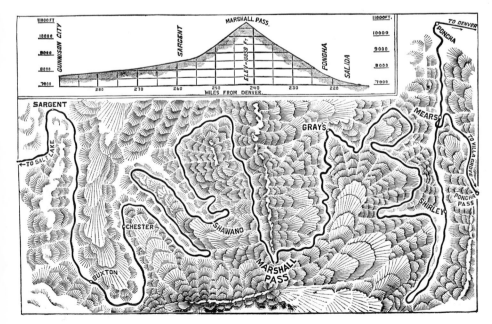

In the panoramic Jackson view above, three little D&RG 2-8-0s are working up Marshall Pass's steep grades with 27 cars and a caboose strung between them. The track in the foreground was negotiated a few minutes earlier — but not the spur, which inexplicably is not connected to the main by a switch. At right, Jackson photographed an 18-car mixed descending through another succession of zigzag loops; three levels of tracks can be seen. 2-8-0 no. 273 provides some braking effort while the train crew "decorates the tops", ready to set hand brakes if needed. (Both photos State Historical Society of Colo.) At left, another 2-8-0 poses on one of the line's innumerable wood trestles, under the shadow of Mt. Ouray. The engine is probably returning down the mountain after having done helper duty on an uphill train. (Museum Collection.)

2708 - IN MARSHAL PASS.

freighting businesses from the new railhead, which soon assumed the character of the now defunct Silver Creek. "One man has already been killed at the new town and things promise to be red hot there for the next two weeks," said the *Review*.

Thus far the railroad had experienced remarkably little labor trouble considering the number of men in its employ. Alexander Hunt was quoted in the Denver *Tribune* saying that the railroad had more men on the payroll than the United States Army. However, of the 32,-000 he cited, 19.000 were actually at work on the Palmer line in Mexico, the narrow gauge Ferrocarril Nacional Mexicano. Another three or four thousand were working for the D&RG in New Mexico, five or six thousand in Colorado, and the remainder in Utah.

It is not surprising that among this many men, some should bear grudges against the railroad. Five men employed as tie cutters on the west slope of Marshall Pass harbored such ill feelings against the railroad that during July they attempted to wreck a train. The men were paid by the tie rather than by the day, and a locomotive spewing the usual hot coal cinders had set a fire on the pass that burned up a pile of ties they had just cut. The railroad, if it did not refuse settlement for the burned ties, was at least slow to make any payment, and the tie cutters, convinced they had been refused, hired two dim-witted teen-age boys, the sons of a nearby resident, to wreck a train. On Sunday, July 16, the boys, Jacob and James Cross, the one 16 years of age, the other 13, went about their task. They had been promised a dollar each, though they were paid only a quarter each. On the steep four per cent down grade they first greased a section of track. Then they began piling spikes, fishplates and finally a telegraph pole on the track. A westbound train managed to stop only a foot from the obstruction. J. R. DeRemer was notified of the attempt, and captured the boys at 3 p.m. that day. They confessed readily and DeRemer went on to capture the five men who had paid them. The boys were held as witnesses, and Sheriff Clark

The top of Marshall Pass provided great vistas of distant valleys and mountain ranges. Here an early passenger train, during the first few years of operation, pauses near the summit for benefit of both passengers and Mr. Jackson, the photographer, while a multi-engined freight toils through the loop visible lower in the valley. (Michael Davis Coll.)

took the five men to Silver Creek for trial.

West of Sargents grade work was continued. At least 1,500 men were at work between Sargents and Gunnison, operating out of fifteen or twenty grading camps. By July 27 all but two and a half miles of grading on the D&RG between those points was completed and the "front" or end of track was four miles west of Crooksville. In Gunnison the railroad company had arranged for building freight houses in the vicinity of the D&RG depot. On July 29 the citizens held a meeting to argue whether a celebration should be planned to greet the railroad. A Mr. Levi proposed that the chairman appoint a committee of

five to collect money for a hearty reception, but Judge Smith objected. If they wanted to come, he said, let them come. When he rode on their cars he had to pay fare· why should he put himself out on the railroad's account? Judge Harlow responded with an eloquent speech, dwelling on the importance of the railroad to the era. "Let us extend our welcome to them," he said; "If they don't appreciate our efforts, it is not our fault." Professor Richardson then spoke in favor of giving a reception to both the Rio Grande and the Denver, South Park & Pacific. The participants agreed.

On August 3 an unfortunate accident occurred at the top of the pass, where the westbound passen-

ger train had paused at the summit. A freight climbing up from Shirley with the throttle wide open ran into the rear car of the passenger train before the engineer could shut off steam, and the jolt pushed the passenger train down the 4 per cent grade on the western slope. Before the startled passenger engineer could halt his train it ran into a construction train that was being switched onto a siding to allow the passenger train to pass. The force of the collision derailed several cars and it was two hours before the line was clear and the passenger train could continue. Fortunately there were no fatalities, although in the first collision Mrs. M. A. Robertson was thrown through a window and apparently suffered some internal

Shortly after completion of the Marshall Pass line, Salida's resident commercial photographer C. H. Clark made a series of photos of the route. Above, Mr. Clark has trained his camera straight down the long tangent leading east from the Pass; snowsheds and water tower are visible in the foreground, while additional snowsheds can be seen in the distance, as the line starts its twisting descent to Salida. Below, the photographer has moved to the other side of the ridge to capture the twisting, undulating snowsheds on film; in the process he also captured the bleak, windswept atmosphere of Marshall Pass. (Both photos, Museum Coll.)

Marshall Pass was equipped with engine, depot and boardinghouse facilities, all integrated with the snowsheds, as shown in the photo above (State Historical Society of Colo. Coll.). A sharp eye will detect the tall and undoubtedly breezy lookout tower, shown in detail in the 1898 view below. The snowsheds had already acquired a veneer of sheet-tin; the sturdy, two-story brick boarding house provided an air of permanence and solidity to the assemblage. (Denver Public Library Western Coll.) On the page opposite, Salida photographer Clark stopped a three-engine freight on one of the line's spindly curved trestles (bridge 17). Actually, the train is headed downgrade, with the helper engines preceding it light; Clark had them stop while the road engine caught up with them for the triple-header photo. (Museum Coll.)

30

injuries. She was taken down to Sargents and left there to recuperate.

Charles Groff, assigned by the D&RG to be their Gunnison agent, arrived there on August 3 along with General Freight Agent Eccles. The two had just come in from the railhead, which was only six miles east of Gunnison. The rate of construction could be measured, they said, by the mile and three-quarters of track laid between 2 p.m. and quitting time that day.

They also reported that all the railroad carpenters were busy building bridges, so work on the D&RG buildings in Gunnison would not begin for at least a week.

Eccles played the usual public relations role, saying there was no reason Gunnison should not replace Denver and Pueblo as distributing point for traffic to the mountain country. He claimed that it was the intention of the company to give Gunnison low rates to encourage shipping and business in the Gunnison country. These were the usual platitudes D&RG officials offered.

Train Time in Gunnison

"What was that?" A half dozen citizens standing at the corner of Main Street and Tumitchi Avenue in Gunnison on the evening of August 5, 1881, stopped in their tracks. The long mournful wail of a locomotive whistle echoed faintly off the hills of the Gunnison River valley for the first time in history. With a field glass or telescope one could see a little diamond stacked engine slowly pushing around the bluff at the east end of J. H. Haverly's ranch. That day a mile and a half of new track and several new bridges had been completed:

Nearer to town, scattered along in black patches between here and the point now occupied by the engine, were hundreds of workmen shoveling and picking as for dear life in work on the grade. Sundown came, but these gangs continued at their work, their lanterns flickering like fire flies over the valley, and steadily drawing nearer to town. There was no longer a doubt as to the sincerity of the

Passenger traffic on the Marshall Pass line in the eighties fluctuated somewhat, but was generally brisk. Handling of a heavier train is clearly shown in the Jackson sequence at right, picturing no. 4 ascending the west side of Marshall. One engine (probably one of the 45 class moguls) comes up first with the two mail and baggage cars (bottom), followed by the coaches and pullmans as a second section, handled by a pair of diamond-stack Baldwins. (Both, State Historical Society of Colo.) Lighter traffic in subsequent years saw a standardized consist as at left — a mail and a baggage, two coaches and a Pullman, pulled by a tenwheeler road engine and C-19 2-8-0 as helper, operated as one section. (Top, Museum Coll.; center, A. M. Payne Coll.) The rare photo at bottom (taken at the Poncha Pass wye) shows that operating practice on the Salida-Alamosa run over Poncha Pass in the nineties was identical — a tenwheeler (no. 174) assisted by a C-19 (no. 408) to the top of the Pass, with five cars. The 408's fireman has just lined up the switch and the 174 will shortly depart down the San Luis Valley for Alamosa, a run that will involve two hours' running over absolutely tangent track with nary a curve. (Museum Coll.)

WEST SIDE MARSHALL PASS

The west side of Marshall was equally as scenic — and as steep — as the east side. Above D&RG 402, the "Shoshone" (one of the big C-19's ordered for Marshall Pass service) poses with a short freight that includes two different versions of the D&RG's through refrigerator cars for "fruit and perishables" (Museum Coll.); while below no. 41 pauses with a construction train a half dozen track levels below the Pass on the horizon beyond (State Historical Society of Colo.).

D&RG's haste to reach Gunnison.

All Saturday morning, August 6, the sound of locomotive whistles and bells echoed through the valley of the Gunnison. They were "voices of civilization" as one resident put it. At 2:25 p.m. tracklayers spiked rails down across main street, and at 2:40 Denver & Rio Grande Railway construction engine 71 gingerly rolled onto the virgin track. Engineer Rice applied the brakes, hauled back on the whistle cord and "let her scream." It was appropriate that this first engine to reach Gunnison, a Class 56 2-8-0 built in 1880, was named the "Pacific Slope."

Oddly enough there was no large crowd to watch the scene, for the thermometer was up in the nineties, and most residents of Gunison had worn themselves out in the morning watching the track and two engines creep towards town along the northern edge of the Mowbray ranch. For those not present the *News-Democrat* described the "remarkable collection of rolling stock" attached to Engine 71. There were "old storm-battered box cars that looked as if they had gone through a hundred railroad wars," their roofs pierced with rusty stovepipes. These veterans were

> sandwiched in with flats and more respectable boxes (box cars). Through the open doors of the latter could be seen bunks, and now and then a clothes line supporting an array of blue and red shirts hung out to dry. This train is known in railroad parlance as "the hotel." It left Poncha Springs last March, and has been making its way hither ever since. In it have been, and for that matter still are, lodged the men who have constructed the road. It is provided with a regular kitchen, a capital cook, a laundry and as has been intimated, sleeping accommodations for all hands. It is in charge of Conductor Sullivan.

Thus the home of the track laying crew came to Gunnison.

That afternoon track was laid on across Main Street to the location staked out for the wye, near where the depot was to be built, and the boarding train moved on down to the meadows, clearing the track for the supply train. With the line clear, Engineer Sheehey hauled back on the throttle and brought his thirty cars of ties and rails charging into town "in style." His engine, the second one to reach Gunnison, was number 41, another Class 56 2-8-0 named the "Grand Canon" after that gorge on the Arkansas River in which the war against the Santa Fe had been fought. Towards sundown, more and more people gathered to gaze at the two trains. The town had been disappointed to learn that the first passenger train would not arrive the same day, but by 3:30 the fact was indisputable, for Engineer Shehey and Conductor Field had telegraphic train orders to take their supply train back to Sargents; thus no passenger train could be out on the single track line.

Sunday, August 7, was no day of rest, according to the *Review:*

> Although the track was laid ... across Main-st. last Saturday afternoon, the lively work of the company was performed on Sunday when its immense army of laborers here was employed putting down side tracks, switches, the Y, and running their Crested Butte branch northward from Bidwell to Virginia-ave., a distance of half a mile. The main track was laid down to Ninth-st. and there was at least a quarter of a mile of cars side-tracked here all that day.

The two construction trains, powered by the same locomotives that had come in Saturday, were in town all day.

A rumor spread during the middle of the day that a passenger train would arrive at 2 p.m., and several hundred people assembled at the cut just southeast of town where the railroad climbed out of the valley onto the little bluff on which the town was built to await it. But the train never came and most of the crowd retreated from the hot sun back to town. A third of them remained, watching the "tracklayers do some of the liveliest work ever before done in the way of railroad building on the continent." The laborers quit work at 6 p.m. and it was some time after that before the last spectators left the scene.

Main street that evening in Gunnison was "one of the most lively, business thoroughfares in Colorado," boasted the *Review:*

> The side walks were almost a solid mass of moving humanity, while the hotels, restaurants, saloons, gambling houses, confectionery establishments, the varieties, etc., were as lively as a sugar cask in fly time. We doubt if Leadville in its palmiest days ever saw a more lively crowd on any of its streets than that surging to and fro Sunday evening on Main-st.

Such was Gunnison's experience in that brief period when it was the "front" of construction on the Denver & Rio Grande.

The following morning, Monday, August 8, 1881, quite a crowd gathered around the depot grounds to await the first train; they were "idly walking along the track or seeking a shelter from the scorching rays of the morning sun." Everyone kept looking to the east and wondering out loud when the train would come. Workmen were busy laying another side track, and their speed and proficiency surprised the townspeople. Engine 77, another Class 56 2-8-0 named the "Rinconada" had brought in another supply train of flat cars loaded with ties and rail, and was standing with steam up to shunt them around when necessary.

The passenger train was expected at 8 a.m., but 8:30 and finally 9 a.m. went by and still the train did not come. The crowd was patient and good humored and expressed a determination, said the newspaper quoting the words of General Grant, to "fight it out on that line if it took all summer." By 9 o'clock a number of the most prominent citizens of Gunnison, together with nearly all the railroad officials in the city, were "standing foolishly by the track," reported the *Daily News Democrat*. Mr. Mellen, the photographer, was out with his camera, and got a few good views of the crowd. Finally the smoke of the train was sighted off to the east, and just at 9:30 the wail of the whistle was heard.

The first passenger train into Gunnison was pulled by Engine 46, the "Badito," engineer George B. Shanley at the throttle and Edward

The Gunnison that the D&RG was rushing to build into looked like this in 1882 — a rough frontier town, with more of a prairie atmosphere than mountain characteristics. Main Street (above) was a wide, dusty, rock-strewn thoroughfare lined with a mixture of frame buildings and substantial stone or brick structures. Intersecting was Tomichi Street (below), less pretentious even than Main Street, but apparently busy enough with its own commercial activity. (Both, Denver Public Library Western Coll.)

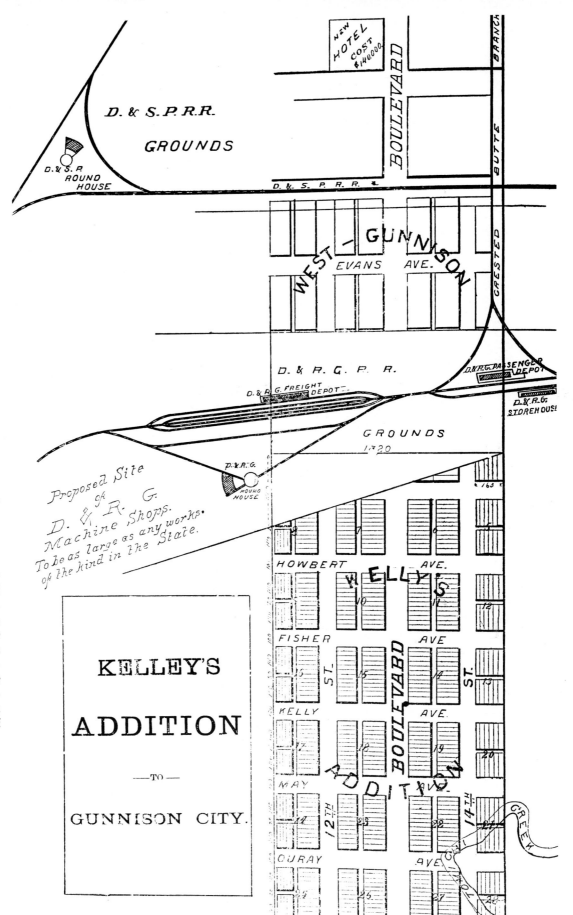

When the D&RG decided to locate their facilities in West Gunnison, the yards were laid out as shown in this ad from the Denver Republican. The Irishman who hoped to profit from the adjacent subdivision seemed unsure of the spelling of his own name — Kelly or Kelley; either way, he was not above platting lots that lay in the middle of Tomichi Creek.

Malloy as fireman, and it towed two coal cars, a baggage car with baggageman E. R. Rhodes, and the the coaches "Saguache" and "Albuquerque" with Barney Gogarty as brakeman and W. H. Brown the conductor. Having unloaded about forty passengers, the train was turned on the wye and about 11:30 a. m. it began the return trip.

At 3:40 that afternoon a special whistled into town carrying General Manager Dodge, General Superintendent G. W. Cushing, Division Superintendent G. M. Kimberly, Chief Engineer McMurtrie, and Trainmaster J. C. Myers. The special was pulled by Engine 35, a Class 38 4-4-0 named "Culebra," built in 1879; it was handled by Engineer Jack Fuller and his train consisted of the cars "Commissary" and "Manitou" with C. L. Hanna as the conductor. The company officials inspected the depot sites and other points of interest and were then driven to their hotels to be waited upon by a congratulatory committee of citizens.

At 3:58 p.m. the regular scheduled passenger train rolled into Gunnison behind Engine 33, a Class 56 2-8-0 built in 1879 and named "Silver Cliff." Behind the locomotive were a baggage car and two passenger cars under Conductor Abbott. The engineer was named Duncan and the fireman was a man named Bowlby.

At 7 p.m. that evening a banquet was given for the railroad officials at the Tabor House. Sponsored by the City Council and the Gunnison Board of Trade (early equivalent of a Chamber of Commerce), it was presided over by ex-governor Crawford, as Mayor Kubler was ill. There were the usual stuffy speeches. Governor Crawford flattered the railroad officials, and in response the railroad attorney, Judge Bennett, flattered the townspeople. The meeting was "very cordial" according to the *News-Democrat*, though it did not stipulate how many fifths of cordiality were consumed.

Once the festivities were over, once Gunnison had settled down and become accustomed to being a railroad town, the Denver & Rio Grande prepared to build onward. First the yards had to be put in

shape for regular operations to the east. Locomotives were temporarily watered by an extension from a nearby flume, until a regular water tank could be erected, but that would have to be done before cold weather froze the flume. As for construction of track, the railroad was immediately interested in completing the line up to Crested Butte, for the mines of that region would not only supply traffic which would bring the railroad revenue, but would also supply coal with which to fuel the engines. The Crested Butte line was temporarily more important than the main line as it offered a nearby source of revenue, whereas the main line offered little revenue short of Salt Lake City. The railroad was now building westward into a vast territory where settlements were few and far between, and much of the land was dry and semi-desert.

In Gunnison a frame depot, a structure 32 x 154 feet, was already up, but the railroad management also planned a stone roundhouse, a freight depot 270 by 40, and machine shops. Even without them the town had the apperance of a railroad center. On August 11 there were four locomotives, a baggage and two passenger cars and 167 box and flat cars reported sitting on sidings in Gunnison. "That will do for a road that laid its track into Gunnison on last Saturday evening," boasted a newspaper. "The screech of three or four locomotives on the D&RG road makes things a little lively on the side tracks near the depots." As the depot in West Gunnison was quite a distance from the older town, two Barlow & Sanderson stages no longer needed over Marshall Pass were pressed into service until two specially ordered 12-passenger horse-drawn buses were received.

The crowded streets of Gunnison became even more crowded on August 12 and intermittently thereafter as a result of troop movements. That day a special passenger train carying five coaches full of soldiers of the 14th Infantry being transferred from Camp Douglas, Utah, to Cantonment Uncompahgre came into town. One soldier had been killed and another injured in an

accident on the west slope of the pass earlier that day. Somehow the front coach parted from the tender and the engine raced ahead of the train before the engineer noticed. Then when he slowed the locomotive the five coaches came racing down the hill to smash into the tender, reducing the platform of the first coach to splinters. Four of six soldiers who were riding on the platform (and who, if playing around, might have pulled open the Miller hook), managed to jump and escape injury. Another, named Miller, was killed in the crash, and the sixth, a man named Weitzel, was so badly injured he was not expected to live. He was taken to the Mullin House after the train limped into Gunnison.

On the rear of that military special, for the accommodation of the officers accompanying the troops, was the first Pullman Palace Sleeping Car that Gunnison had seen. Four days later, on August 16, the first mail car arrived in Gunnison. Furthermore, the telegraph line was now in service, having been completed into Gunnison on August 13. The telegraph office was set up temporarily in a box car on a siding near the depot.

Around the depot in Gunnison a passerby could see every type of vehicle and a great variety of business being transacted. Said the *Review* on August 20:

From early morning until the setting of the sun can be seen at the railroad a lively crowd of people composed of railway employees, merchants, business men, freighters, teamsters, etc., all busily engaged in the work before them. The business of unloading freight cars, of loading merchandise, household goods, machinery, etc., into wagons, gives that portion of town an appearance only witnessed at a live railroad town. For the past week the daily average of freight cars over the road here has been forty or 280 a week. We learn, however, that both passenger and freight business on the road is rapidly increasing, all of which goes to prove that Gunnison is to be one of the most important points west of the range.

In fact the railroad was reported

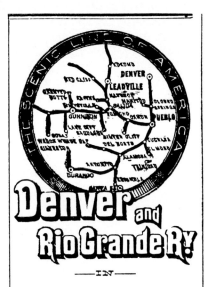

What the photo above lacks in clarity is atoned for by its rarity — it shows one of the first passenger trains in Gunnison, the depot new, the track not yet ballasted, the yards in the distance still under construction. The little Baldwin 2-8-0 is pulling two flat-roofed baggage cars and a pair of early-style (duck bill roof) coaches. Later a spur was laid past the vast La Veta Hotel, and a ticket office established in the corner of the Building (below). For many years the passenger trains stopped here, and an open observation car was attached to the train for the run through the Black Canon. (Both photos, Denver Public Library Western Coll.) Pushing west from Gunnison, the D&RG anticipated great things, and was not bashful about advertising all the line's wondrous attributes and accomplishments-to-be — as is shown in this ad (left) that appeared in the Gunnison Review-Press in 1883.

As soon as the Railroad reached Gunnison, a line was quickly run 28 miles north to Crested Butte, for a very good reason — some of the best locomotive coal in the west. Above, no. 278 pauses at the Anthracite coal breaker (State Historical Society of Colo.); below, no. 34 at the new Crested Butte depot (Denver Public Library Western Coll.).

to be making from $4,000 to $6,0 daily on freight alone.

The impact could be seen on t town, as the *Review* indicated:

The Mullin patch is daily being dotted with new buildings, capital is being invested, new business houses are constantly opening, fine residences are being built, new comers are buying lots, real estate has doubled in the past ten days, miles of freight cars are to be seen along the side tracks, forty car loads of freight come in daily, and hundreds of teams are constantly loading up goods at the depot. The "patch" is booming with business.

Gunnison meanwhile had be bragging that she would soon sp *five* railroads, and was promp chided on this claim by the ri Gothic *Miner*. Sure, said the *Min* there was the D&RG, the Sou Park, the South Park's propos Ohio Creek Extension, the D&I Lake City Branch, and the D&I Crested Butte Branch, all except t first yet to be built. That wou make five railroads. "Don't it asked the *Miner* impudently.

The Gunnison *Review* took the defense, saying that aside fr the D&RG and the South Park, t other narrow gauge lines, which did not specify, were "reaching c from Denver for the wealth of t great Gunnison," and a wealthy c poration, again unspecified, w pushing work on a line from Pue west. "Yes, Mr. Miner, we soon pect five lines of railroad here, t counting them as you are countir the number may possibly reach teen or twenty." The *Review* we on to predict that Gunnison wou become the great metropolis of t western slope, the Denver of t west. "It will be as natural for tra and traffic to center here as it is water to flow down hill," conclud the *Review*.

It certainly seemed that Gun son was prospering. A frame freig depot was under construction a by September 2, Agent Groff w prepared to sell through passeng tickets to any point reached by r in the United States. Tickets Denver were priced at $23.70.

On September 10, 1881, an e cursion of businessmen depart

from Denver for Gunnison, arriving there at 3 a.m. on Sunday, September 11. The hotels were full and there were no accommodations, and most of them were not pleased with the situation at all. Many spent their time fishing and went home with nice strings of trout, but Gunnison had not made the best impression.

Other incidents in September did not show the town's better side. On September 12 two young girls accompanied by a woman known as Frankie arrived by train and were taken to a bagnio in the red light district on the north side of town. Shortly thereafter Sheriff Clark received a frantic telegram from the girls' relatives in Grand Rapids, Michigan, and hurried out to the bawdy house to rescue them. He found them in tears, but otherwise apparently unharmed, being consoled by the other girls there. The two girls claimed to have come to Gunnison with Frankie to take jobs as domestics, but Frankie, who had a good reputation in Michigan, apparently had other ideas. Sheriff Clark lodged the girls in the Tabor House and when notified, their relatives telegraphed that they would come for them immediately.

Gunnison also experienced its first race trouble that month, when a mob attacked Mr. L. Sing, who having arrived from California, had set up a laundry on Main Street. It was Gunnison's first "agitation" of the "Chinese question," according to the *Free Press*, whose editor commented on the irony of Anglo, German, Irish and "African" citizens of Gunnison trying to oust "foreign" competition. It seemed likely that some members of the mob assaulting the laundry owner were more recent immigrants to America than he. After being beaten several times, Mr. Sing pulled a revolver and fired in the air, which only seemed to enrage his attackers. At that point local law officers intervened and he was taken to jail, "as much, it is presumed, for his own protection as anything else," said the *Free Press*. But in the end it appeared to be the "anything else" that counted, for Sing was convicted and fined five dollars and costs for discharging a revolver within the corporate limits of Gunnison while his attackers got off scot free.

Some idea of enterprise in Gunnison at this time can be gleaned from a list of firms published in the October 2 *Free Press*: four hotels, seven lodging houses, thirty saloons, four drug stores, four livery stables, five dance halls, twenty-two restaurants, one theatre, four general merchandise houses, three shoemakers' shops, three harness shops, four wholesale liquor houses, three produce and commission merchants, four freighters' corrals, three paint shops, three furniture stores, one stationery and notion store, one auction house, eight blacksmith shops, four carpenter shops, eight groceries, three bakeries, seven laundries, one second-hand store, one gunsmith's shop, nine dry goods and clothing stores, four barber shops, three hardware stores, two cigar factories, three watchmakers and jewelers, seven dressmakers and milliners, one tailor, two banks, four meat markets, three printing offices, five lumber yards, one planing mill, two real estate offices, two candy factories, two breweries, two transfer lines, three coal dealers, one soda bottling establishment, three assay offices, one boot and shoe store, five hay and grain merchants, and two forwarders. The number of saloons is perhaps an indication of the drinking habits of Americans on the frontier in the 1880s, in an age of limited entertainments. Unfortunately the *Free Press* editor chose to omit a listing of the red light establishments on the north side of town, so that one can only speculate at their number.

On October 7, news reached Gunnison from Denver that negotiations which were in progress in New York City for the D&RG to purchase the South Park line from the Union Pacific had finally fallen through, and the D&RG negotiators had left for Colorado. Businessmen in Gunnison were much relieved, hoping the competition between two separate lines (presuming the tortoise-tracked South Park ever reached Gunnison) would keep rates lower than if the D&RG owned both lines. "It is the best kind of news for Gunnison that we have had for some time," exulted one citizen. He went on to speculate that the deal had fallen through because Sidney Dillon, president of the UP, made abandonment of the planned connection with Salt Lake a *sine qua non* of sale of the South Park. Perhaps the Burlington and even the Sante Fe and Southern Pacific were discouraging the Rio Grande from the purchase on those conditions, hoping to benefit from a line which would compete with the UP between Denver and Ogden. The Burlington was particularly anxious for a connection, for through a pooling arrangement in Omaha, the UP had an axe over its head, with which the UP was trying to stop the Burlington from reaching Denver with its own trackage. But if the Burlington could connect at Denver with a through D&RG — Central Pacific line to the Pacific Coast, it would presumably obtain enough traffic to be able to sacrifice its share of the Omaha pool, and tell the UP to peddle its papers.

As for the Central Pacific, it was faced with a monopolistic junction with the UP at Ogden and would welcome a competing connection, for at the same time the Central Pacific management was irritated by UP construction of the Oregon Short Line towards Oregon, invading a CP preserve. In a sense, the Rio Grande seemed to hold, in 1881, a key to the establishment of a system of transcontinental lines which would compete with the UP from Omaha to the Pacific Coast, with Gunnison right in the middle, or so it seemed to businessmen in Gunnison. No wonder they were so optimistic.

Throughout that fall the D&RG construction crews continued work on both the main line towards the Black Canon and the branch to Crested Butte, and although men were occasionally transferred from the main line to speed completion of the Crested Butte branch to the north, grading west of Gunnison never entirely ceased. It had begun way back in April, when spurred by the appearance of South Park grading crews in the vicinity of Gunnison, D&RG men went to work to secure the approaches to the Black Canon. Palmer was not going to be caught napping again in competition for a gorge wide enough

The Black Canon soon became a major tourist attraction, and the tourists at right (or perhaps they're merely railroad dignitaries) are gazing upwards (while little mogul no. 13 simmers on the main) at the scene below — the Curecanti Needle, just across the narrow stream-bed from their track, and thrusting a thousand feet or more into the sky. The fame of the Curecanti Needle was assured when the D&RG elected to engrave it on the road's fancy new herald, where it was to remain until the 1920's. Other scenes in the Canon are portrayed on the opposite page: top, Jackson's little photographic special stopped just beyond Bridge "B"; lower left, a freight at Crystal River Bridge, where the line turned away from the Gunnison and up a side canyon to Cimarron; and lower right, a very early special posed at Chipeta Falls, deep in the Canon. The flatcar for viewing was not an unusual appendage when a line was just opened. (Lower left opp., Richard Ronzio Coll.; lower right opp., Michael Davis Coll.; all others, Museum Coll.)

Biggest engines used through the Black Canon for years were the 400-series class C-19, later renumbered in the 340 series; the Museum's no. 346 is an example of the class. Above no 404, the "Sevier" (later no. 344), is shown at Cedar Creek, on the west side of Cerro Summit. (Philip Ronfor Coll.) No. 95, below, is reputed to have drawn the first excursion train through the Canon. A neat little straight-stacked eight-wheeler turned out by Baldwin in 1880 as the "Embudo", it was soon replaced by the heavier tenwheelers and eventually sold off to a predecessor of the Atlantic Coast Line. (Richard Kindig Coll.)

for only one railroad, as he had along the Arkansas River. Much of the surveying in the upper Black Canon had to be done from boats anchored by ropes. After some preliminary work west of Gunnison, grading crews began excavating in earnest in the middle of June.

Some of the grading contractors on the Gunnison River and Black Canon line had worked on the construction over Marshall Pass, such as Carrico & Fay, McGavock & Tate, and J. J. Cummings. Others were new contractors, such as W. L. Hoblitzell & Company, Hammond, Hendricks & Company, and Dunbar & Shafer. The railroad itself employed more than a dozen civil engineers to supervise the work of the grading contractors, among them R. L. Engle, John Sheldon, W. H. Linn, J. H. Gunder, W. G. Heinsler, and the ever present DeRemer. It was difficult work; the Black Canon portion of the line was as difficult as any construction encountered in the whole Rio Grande system.

W. L. Hoblitzell's contract for the section roughly from Kezar to Lake Junction—though no such points existed at the time work was begun —was among the first awarded, and it was dated June 6. From the very beginning the line westward from Gunnison seemed plagued with troubles, not all of them of an engineering nature.

On August 11, five days after the end of track had reached Gunnison, a Caraco & Fay grading crew was blasting rock from the grade just west of a camp called Soap Creek, which meant that they were near the mouth of the Black Canon. The crew was using as their explosive an unfamiliar and nasty liquid called nitroglycerine, and it detonated while they were handling it. The foreman, Sweeny, was blown into the stream, and his body disappeared, perhaps under a rock fall. One Negro on the grading crew had his head, left shoulder and side mangled and bruised by flying rock, and his left arm broken, and he died in an hour. Another Negro grader, Tom Cunningham who was standing just as close, was blown fifty feet away, but was unharmed. One of the other men had an arm blown off. The

Black Canon had begun to take its toll.

By September 10, the D&RG together with a land owner named G. H. Kezar had laid out a townsite fourteen miles down the river below Gunnison. Named after Mr. Kezar, the new townsite was laid out in fourteen blocks, and there were already five saloons and a well-stocked general store, though the end of track had not yet reached that far.

Meanwhile the railroad company was busy upgrading its Marshall Pass line. By September 17, the D&RG had completely ballasted the track from Salida to Gunnison, and the trainmaster expected to cut the running time between the two points by an hour. In Gunnison, a man named Russell was awarded the contract to build the six stone stalls of the roundhouse. The building was planned for the addition of more stalls when needed, perhaps a total of sixteen.

Although by the middle of October, 1881, many of the graders working on the main line had been transferred to the Crested Butte Branch, enough were still at work in the Black Canon to prove a source of trouble, especially the Irish and the Italians.

The trouble broke out on Sunday, October 9. As might be expected, it began at a saloon located two miles from the Number 3 Hoblitzell grading camp. An Irishman had bought a bottle of whisky and bet the Italian grading foreman, Mike Soso, that he couldn't drink it. Soso did, but under the influence of so much liquor went wild, pulled a knife and stabbed an Irish bystander named Shaw. The three Irishmen who had been in the saloon ran for their camp, chased by Italians firing at them. After dark a strong party of Irish returned to "arrest" Soso, and after an exchange of fire in which no one was hurt, they suceeded.

At 8 a.m. Monday morning a hundred or more excited Italians marched on Camp No. 5 to free the prisoner. Colonel Hoblitzell was absent, but one of his assistants, T. F. McCardell, met the mob a half mile from Camp No. 5, agreed to release Soso, and calmed the Italians.

On Tuesday morning, McCardell again started for the Italian camp, this time to get the men to work, and met another mob of Italians marching on Camp No. 5. They threatened to kill him unless he paid them all off immediately. McCardell refused any settlement until pay day and retreated to Camp 5, ordering the Italians not to follow him. They followed anyway, but were met at Camp 5 by fifty armed Irishmen. Then it was the Italians' turn to retreat, and although McCardell tried to stop it, the Irishmen chased them all the way back to Camp 3. Fearing for their lives, the Italians scattered in all directions, some fleeing to the hills, some swimming the Gunnison River, with about thirty being captured and disarmed by the Irish. There were also reports that the Irish had set fire to some of the tents and buildings at Camp No. 3. McCardell finally got control of his men, and no one was harmed.

But that was only the beginning of the trouble in the Black Canon. At 9 a.m. on Thursday, October 27, an Italian-speaking Austrian nipper or tool carrier named Theophile walked into W. L. Hoblitzell's office at Camp No. 5 and demanded his pay. Hoblitzell's policy was to pay men off only on ten days' notice, so he refused, saying that he could make no exceptions. He was having trouble understanding the Austrian's broken English anyway. Hoblitzell returned to examining papers with McCardell, leaving the Austrian muttering to himself outside.

Shortly thereafter, Theophile entered the store adjacent to the office, still complaining, and Hoblitzell, annoyed by his persistence, told him to leave or he would be put out. Hoblitzell then proceeded to try to usher Theophile out, and the two got into a fight in which the Austrian seemed to be getting the worst of it. McCardell and a Negro worker intervened and separated the two men, and Theophile agreed to leave. But while Hoblitzell was straightening his clothes, Theophile turned on the door sill and fired point blank with a revolver variously described as a Colt, Smith & Wesson, or English bulldog. As Hoblit-

zell staggered back, Theophile ran, threatening anyone who tried to stop him. Seizing a double-barreled shotgun from his tent, he vanished.

Hoblitzell managed to walk back into his office and remove his coat. A Dr. Stroud who happened to be in the vicinity came over to treat him. The bullet had entered Hoblitzell's right breast between the fifth and sixth ribs. W. P. Coghill, the storekeeper, mounted immediately and rode to Gunnison for Dr. Latham, making the twenty-two mile ride in less than two hours. Dr. Latham headed out immediately to the grading camp.

A posse of about a hundred men from the grading camps started out after the assailant, but failed to catch him. Colonel Hoblitzell remained conscious and talked with J. R. DeRemer about jointly inspecting the line in a couple of days. Mr. Carico came in the Hoblitzell smoked a cigar with him. But the medical prognosis was very unfavorable.

Later that day Assistant Chief Engineer DeRemer and the grading contractor J. M. Carico went on into Gunnison and had a "wanted" poster printed up:

$1,000 REWARD!

Ben Theophile, sometimes called "Pete," claiming to be an Austrian, but speaking Italian, wantonly shot and dangerously wounded W. L. Hoblitzell, at Camp Hoblitzell, twenty-two miles below Gunnison, Oct. 27, 1881. Theophil is a short, thick-set man, dark complexion, black hair, high cheek bones, and smiles continually while in conversation. Wore a black mustache and thin chin whiskers at the time of the shooting. Wore also dark clothing, and heavy nailed boots and a close-fitting cap. About five feet seven inches in height. Has been in Colorado several years, working on railroads. I will pay five hundred dollars reward for his capture.

J. R. DeRemer

We will also pay five hundred dollars for the same purpose.

Carico & Fay

Meanwhile, DeRemer notified Hoblitzell's wife and daughter in Colorado Springs, and R. F. Weitbrec at the railway offices there called a special train to take them to the grading camp, with telegraphic orders to division superintendents to clear the line for the special, and to the engineer to run as fast as was safe. Mrs. Hoblitzell and her daughter left Colorado Springs at 7:25 p.m., but were not in time, for Hoblitzell died at 9 p.m. while they were still somewhere east of Marshall Pass.

At about 8 p.m. Sheriff Yule arrived at the camp and exchanged his exhausted horse for a mule. He then recruited two deputies, Peter Smith and S. A. Albright, and just before Hoblitzell died, left in pursuit of Theophile. They stopped at all three of the Carrico & Fay camps, but no one had seen the Austrian. Then en route down the grade to the first Hutchinson camp, they saw a campfire off to the right. It could have been Theophile's, but if it was, it might also mean an ambush, so the three rode on by to Hutchinson's camp and inquired there. Receiving a negative response, the trio rested fifteen minutes and then headed back east. They rested again for 45 minutes at a ranch en route, and just before daybreak saddled up and headed back towards the site of the campfire they had seen earlier that night. Just at daybreak as they approached the vicinity of the campfire a man stepped into the road. He had been hunting and had a rabbit in his right hand, a shotgun in his left. Albright, who was riding out front, recognized him and said, "Hello, Pete." The Austrian remembered Albright as a fellow worker, replied, and when Theophile reached up to shake Albright's proferred hand, Albright grabbed Theophile's hand and yelled to the Sheriff, "Cover him George." The sheriff leveled his Colt .45 and seized Theophile's shotgun and the revolver stuck in the Austrian's belt. Theophile was then made to mount behind Albright with the Sheriff and other deputy following right behind.

Sheriff Yule knew from what Carico and DeRemer had said that feeling against the Austrian was running high—Hoblitzell had been popular with at least some of his employees. When the trio with their prisoner approached the Hoblitzell

grading camp, groups of excited men gathered along the road. The sheriff and his deputies put the spurs to their mounts and dashed through the crowd before anyone could stop them. "Stop, bring the son of a bitch here! Give him to us," some of the mob yelled, but the sheriff and his deputies safely reached Gunnison with their prisoner at 4 p.m., avoiding the main streets and lodging the prisoner, thoroughly shackled, in the cage in the county jail.

Several D&RG officials, probably including DeRemer, and several contractors, probably including Carico, demanded an immediate preliminary examination, and the District Attorney agreed, with the hearing called at Justice Harlow's court at 8:30 p.m. But no one appeared to press charges, and Sheriff Clark and District Attorney Goudy began to suspect that the railroad men had decided to take matters into their own hands. Having decided that even the jail might not be a safe place to hold Theophile, Mr. Goudy proposed keeping the Austrian securely shackled in the court room above the jail. Sheriff Clark agreed, and Theophile was moved upstairs, guarded there by Clark himself.

At midnight, Clark heard steps on the stairs, and thinking it was an extra guard whom he had earlier summoned (or so he claimed), he opened the door and was confronted with half dozen cocked pistols held by a crowd of men in black masks. Other masked men entered the room, found Theophile, his legs shackled, sleeping on a bench in the back, put a rope around his neck, and dragged him out. The lynch mob locked the sheriff in the court room, and he could hear Theophile screaming and choking as they dragged him by the rope, his body bumping down the stairs.

When Sheriff Clark's wife found him and freed him, he followed the trail through the snow eastward to the old Kelmel & Allison Livery Stable on Tumitchi Avenue, where he found the bruised and still bleeding body of Theophile hanging from the livery sign. It appeared that the Austrian had been dead even before he had been strung up.

The Gunnison *News-Democrat* was highly incensed at this example

of lynch law: "Good God," exclaimed the paper, "has it come to this, that a railroad monopoly can override all the business of law and order which a respectable city has created for its own protection?" Surely, the editor conceded, the murder of Colonel Hoblitzell was a lamentable piece of business,

> but is that any reason why a party of railroad men should turn this fair town of ours into a slaughter house? Have you no pride, men of Gunnison, that you will permit this bloody business to go on without a protest? We pay for a judge and justice in this city, and if a party of lawless men, who do not own a penny's worth of property in the city, are to be allowed to trample both under their feet, then the sooner we give up our city charter, and let the valley settle back into the barbarous state in which it was found by the first white settlers, the better.

As might be expected, the perpetrators of lynch law in Gunnison were never punished. The Black Canon of the Gunnison had increased its toll.

But work went on, not only in the Black Canon but on Marshall Pass and on the Crested Butte line. On the pass, carpenters had been at work since October building snowsheds at the summit and other vulnerable points that needed such protection.

The Crested Butte line at this time was rapidly nearing completion. As of October 12 the tracklayers were working at a rate of a mile and a half per day, and by November 16 had reached within two miles of the town. At 11:59 a.m. on Monday, November 21, 1881, the first D&RG train rolled into Crested Butte. "With a rapidity that is astonishing even to those accustomed to see it, the track was extended to the coal shutes at the west end of the town, and the first load of Crested Butte coal was put upon the cars," commented the *Crested Butte Republican*; "NOVEMBER 21 will ever be a 'red letter' day in the history of Crested Butte."

On Thanksgiving Day, 1881, D&RG Engine 68, a class 56 2-8-0 named "Vermejo" pulled the train for Denver out of town using a tender of Crested Butte coal as a test of that product. Later, Division Superintendent Myers at Salida telegraphed the general superintendent of the D&RG that it "proved to be a success; it burns cleaner and longer than the Canon City coal and makes lots of steam." By November 30, the D&RG was daily shipping over 80 tons of coal for its own use, mostly in locomotives. The Crested Butte branch was already proving its worth.

On the main line below Gunnison, most of the grading to Soap Creek (later to be called Sapinero after a Ute Indian chief) had been done by a railroad company force under the supervision of Assistant Engineer George Rankin, rather than by contractors. From Soap Creek through the Black Canon and the Cimarron Canon to Cedar Creek Summit in the Squaw Hills (later named Cerro Summit), the grading had been contracted out to six different companies. Some of the contractors had found it necessary first to build wagon roads to get their equipment in to their project site.

From Cerro Summit west to Montrose, much of the grading had been contracted out to the huge Mormon firm of Hammond & Hendircks, and by November 12 they had the work completed from the summit to the junction of the Uncompahgre and Gunnison Rivers. Much of their work was light grading, requiring no blasting and merely the use of horse-drawn scrapers. From Soap Creek nearly to the Utah line one traveling west would encounter these grading camps every few miles along the route. It was an impressive sight.

At the same time this work was going on, Meyer & Simmons, with Dunbar & Shafer as subcontractors, were at work on a branch line which followed the Lake Fork of the Gunnison up to Lake City. But after much of the heavy work had been done, construction of this line was suspended.

Altogether the eight contracting firms at work here employed 1,200 men, 150 alone working for Clark Lipe & Company, most of the force being Italian.

The work became more difficult as winter came on, but was never entirely suspended. Even train service over Marshall Pass became erratic; as early as November 13 snow on the pass was interfering with train operations, for not all the snowsheds were yet finished. Passengers arriving at Gunnison complained of having suffered considerably from hunger during the delay, but got scant sympathy from the Gunnison *News-Democrat*. "No person should attempt to cross the range at this season without first providing himself with a day's rations," admonished the newspaper.

Such hardships were not advertised by the Denver & Rio Grande Railway; the company's publicity claimed that

Its passenger trains are equipped throughout with Westinghouse Automatic Brakes, and Miller Platforms and Couplers. These appliances, not possessed by any other mountain line, are the only ones which keep a train at all times under perfect control, insure smoothness of motion, and the nearest approach to absolute immunity from danger.

Its coaches are models of elegance and comfort. Handsomely upholstered chair-cars, with *partitioned* toilet rooms, are run on day trains, and three magnificent Pullman Sleepers are attached to night trains, supplying ample and luxurious accommodations for its myriad of patrons.

Meanwhile trainmaster J. C. Myers was in Gunnison on November 16 and that evening submitted to an interview with a *News-Democrat* reporter whom he told that the Marshall Pass line would be kept open all winter, more than a mile of snowsheds being complete with more still under construction. "It will naturally take some time for the company to learn where the worst cuts are," said Myers, "but for a new road this one is managed very creditably." He said that recent delays had been exaggerated by the press, and anyway were due more to accidents than to snow, a delay on November 14 being due to the derailment of an engine, and that of the 15th due to the eastern train being five hours late. However on the 16th a snow-

storm on the pass tied up the westbound passenger train right at the summit, with the line ahead blocked by three freights stuck in the three-foot deep snow. Before the line was cleared by a push plow, a second passenger train was brought to a halt. A lot of rather frightened passengers were happy to be safely in Gunnison that night.

On New Year's Day 1882 there occurred a further inconvenience to passengers, for a roaring fire consumed Joseph Sargent's hotel. Travelers would have to do temporarily without the convenience of that meal stop.

The last month of 1881 did not pass without further trouble in the Black Canon. On December 12 a workman at Sam Tate's grading camp was badly injured when a premature explosion of an explosive cap tore off his right hand and his left thumb, as well as putting out one eye and cutting him around the throat and chin. And that same evening a one-story stone hotel and saloon run by Sam Randall near the headquarters of McGavock & Tate was dynamited deliberately. Several men were apparently injured, and the *News-Democrat* speculated that it was the work of some of Randall's personal enemies.

In February, 1882, the *Daily News-Democrat* raised eyebrows in Gunnison by quoting a Kansas City *Times* article to the effect that the Chicago, Burlington & Quincy had bought the D&RG. It speculated that perhaps the AT&SF was acting with the Burlington in order to outflank Mr. Gould. The D&RG line to Utah would probably be completed at the same time as the Burlington's line into Denver, and a third rail "could be put down on the Denver & Rio Grande's Utah extension in a few weeks," said the newspaper. But the rumor proved to be false.

Gunnison had continued to grow and was now a respectable city of 4,000. The east and west towns were growing together towards the brick school house which had wisely been built between them. Tumitchi Avenue was the main connection between the two towns.

"Alighting from the train of the D&RG railroad, the newcomer to

Gunnison will find himself on the platform of a depot four times as large as the buildings which serve for depot purposes in towns of the same size in the east," claimed the *Daily News Democrat* on February 18, 1882:

> On both sides, to the east and west, he will see immense freight houses, their long and broad platforms covered with freight from all parts of the Union. Two stages and half a dozen smaller hacks will be found awaiting the passengers from the train. The cries of rival hotel runners will awaken in his ears the familiar din of an Eastern city railway station . . .

In town, brick and stone buildings were going up among the wooden ones, such as the Miner's Exchange Bank. In the railroad yards, the D&RG stone roundhouse was under construction, and another such structure was being erected for the South Park line. There was also a D&RG construction company warehouse, a stone machine shop was being built, and the Rio Grande maintained a timber yard employing fifty men in framing bridge and building timbers for the line to the west.

Trains continued to rush westward with steel, spikes, bolts, splice bars and ties. Sometimes they hurried too much. On Saturday, February 18, such haste cost three casualties. A westward freight had been cut into three sections to ascend Marshall Pass and the first section had stopped to switch in the gloom of the nine-hundred foot long double tracked snowshed at the summit. Downgrade, the double-headed westbound passenger train had passed the third and second sections of the freight and was following a work train ascending the pass. At the entrance to the summit snowshed the work train switched into the siding and the passenger worked slowly into the pitch-black, smoke-filled shed on the main track. Suddenly the engineer saw the caboose of the first section of the freight ahead of him in the center of the shed, whistled "down brakes" and threw the locomotive into reverse. But before stopping, the double-header passenger smashed in the whole end of the caboose, knock-

ing over the stove and setting the caboose curtains on fire. Freight conductor Frank Seeley was climbing up from the caboose onto the box car ahead when the collision occurred, and the front edge of the caboose roof smashed into the top of the box car, smashing both of his legs beneath the knees. The brakeman had a foot and ankle mangled and the freight fireman, Dick Bowlby, tried to jump and was pinned between the engine and tender. The injured were rushed back to Salida by a special train, with Seeley in considerable pain begging his companions to shoot him. In Salida, doctors worked to save his legs, with unknown results.

Such accidents did not noticeably delay construction. By February 21, 400,000 ties, enough for 128 miles of track, were en route to Gunnison, and twenty-three car loads of steel were parked on sidings in town. Down in the Black Canon, 1,100 men continued to chip away at the grade, and the company expected to resume track-laying in March.

General Passenger Agent F. C. Nims came into Gunnison on February 23 and went on up to Crested Butte, returning on the following day. Before returning to Denver on February 25 he gave a *News-Democrat* reporter the usual blarney about Gunnison being the "coming city of Western Colorado." He also said that there was "no railroad line in America, or in the world, which for scenery can compare with this." He had already adopted the slogan, "Scenic Line of America" in advertising the Rio Grande.

The holiday of July 4 was celebrated by residents of Gunnison on an excursion to Crested Butte via the railroad. The engine, "handsomely" decorated with flags and evergreens, pulled out of the station at 8:30 a.m. and puffed towards Mount Carbon and the Anthracite Range. To the left was the clear, sparkling water of the Gunnison, edged with groups of Cottonwood trees and clumps of willows, with hills sparsely covered with spruce off to the right. "The train goes thundering up the valley, through the gorges, passing by huge granite walls which it was necessary to cut down to build the road," recalled

one participant. The excursion train stopped at Fisher's long enough for the engine to take water, then raced on through Jack's Cabin and Howeville, arriving in Crested Butte at 10 a.m.

There the excursionists were met by a crowd of the town's residents, and all paraded up and down the principal streets in Crested Butte. From noon to 2:30, dinner was served in the newly built Elk Mountain House, the menu consisting of a staggering 82 offerings. There were foot, pony and horse races, target shooting and other amusements to occupy the afternoon hours, and at 9 p.m. the hundred tired Gunnisonians boarded the train for the return trip.

Out on the main line, the railhead had reached Soap Creek at the entrance to the Black Canon on July 5. A *News-Democrat* correspondent who rode the accommodation train there was not much impressed with the scenery as far as Kezar, where the train stopped a half hour for supper. Not being hungry he wandered through the settlement, his explorations turning up "many saloons, a grocery" and nothing much else. After looking up a druggist friend who had moved there from Gunnison, Correspondent Jones climbed aboard the train for the run to the "front".

The scenery began to improve. The passengers could "see the engine ahead, then disappear and the middle portion of the train come in view as we followed the serpentine meanderings of the river." Soap Creek was most unimpressive:

> I found out a fact which would go far to upset the theories of the prohibitionists — that the people of Soap Creek live on whiskey. There is no other visible means of living, as among eight or nine saloons, only one combines the business of a restaurant.

Neither was the origin of the name apparent, as Mr. Jones "did not see any soap, and had to take a dry wash before leaving." Jones spent an uncomfortable night in a tent which was two feet short of meeting the ground, and as he was the outside man with only a small piece of old tent canvas for a blanket, he was exposed to the night cold. Besides, some of the boys came in rather late "suffering from the weather, and there was a good deal of profane language . . ." It was so cold that after getting out of bed twice to have a smoke, Jones gave up the idea of getting any sleep and impatiently awaited the sunrise.

That morning he talked with construction engineer Engle, who told him that tracklaying was progressing at about a mile a day, with 2,200 ties per mile, and that the line was well ballasted.

Another man who recalled Black Canon construction was the newly hired telegrapher from California, Jefferson Allen. Having arrived at the "front" near a spire of rock called the Curecanti Needle on July 17th, Allen found space in the canon so limited that he had to set up his instruments using rocks for a table and chair. There was simply no place to set up the tent and furniture with which the railroad had supplied him.

A writer named Ripley Hitchcock also visited the end of track while it was in the Black Canon, riding out among ties on a flat car in a supply train as it crept down the Gunnison:

Presently the hills along the river grew higher and more precipitous, the mesas gave way to crumbling crags, and with a farewell shriek from the engine, the train thundered out of sunshine into gloom. Frowning cliffs rose straight up from the track on one side, and on the other the gray river brawled along the foot of the opposing precipice. Mountains of reddish gray rock towered aloft on either hand, veined with white, and seamed with fissures worn with the passage of ages. Here, great bowlders literally overhung the track, and again, there were dark caves or fleecy cascades above or the grim canon walls were almost exactly vertical from their giddy summits to the ribbon of steel and the river at their base.

Hitchcock recalled earlier phases of construction, when "surveyors picked their way through on ice in the winter," when "men and even horses and wagons were lowered down steep slopes by ropes, and workmen wielded drill and hammer, hanging by ropes until they had blasted out a foothold."

Hitchcock stopped at the boarding or "hotel" train, which was parked on the siding opposite the Curecanti Needle, in the canyon's shadow.

Here was the temporary home of four hundred men. A little beyond was the working train at the very end of the rails. All along the dump or road-bed, gangs of men were busily unloading and placing ties and rails, or leveling the surface with exactness. Presently a whistle blew. Six o'clock had come, and the men leaving their tasks scrambled aboard the flat cars and the train rumbled back to the "hotel on wheels." Long before the cars stopped, the men were hustling each other like a flock of stampeded sheep in a wild race for supper. The seats were limited in number, the laborers many, and none had any idea of waiting for "second table" . . . The next morning would be time enough for soap and water. There were swarthy Italians, Irishmen with carroty locks, men of a score of nationalities, begrimed, tattered, gnawed at by the appetite given by labor in the bracing Colorado air, all brethren in a purely animal instinct, a ravenous desire of satisfying hunger. They swarmed into the old freight cars which had been fitted up with long planks for benches and tables. On the latter were tin pannikins, iron knives and forks, and pewter spoons. Mounds of coarse bread, pans of some strange stew, and pots of rank black tea appeared and disappeared before these lusty trenchermen. Words were not wasted. Every act had a bearing upon the business of satisfying hunger. A railroad navvy hungry and tired has "no time for nonsense." One by one they rose from the table. There was nothing to be said. They had been fed and for the time they were content. But presently the social instinct reasserted itself. They lighted black pipes and drew together. Some rudely mended their garments, in company, and others produced dirty cards, or gathered to talk. A few clambered into the narrow board bunks in the cars and drew their blankets up over aching limbs.

It was a glimpse of a hard cheerless life that I had had, but as I turned to go back to the construction train some one struck up a rollicking Irish song and others joined until the canon walls gave back the chorus.

Hitchcock noted that there were special dangers to working in such a canyon: "A little time before, two men were swept away by the rapid current of the river, others had been killed by the overhanging rocks." But at least they did not have Indian trouble to plague them, as did other lines in the West.

In the succeeding weeks the tracklayers laid their rails to the mouth of the Cimarron, then on the grade up the Cimarron Canon by which the railroad escaped the even more precipitous gorge of the lower reaches of the Black Canon. The end of track was spiked down in the townsite of Cimarron on August 9, and at 8:30 a.m. on Sunday, August 13, 1882, the first passenger train to go through the Black Canon pulled out of Gunnison. It consisted of a baggage car, two coaches, and four of the open observation cars, hauled by Engine 95, a little 4-4-0 named Embuda. William Duncan was the engineer, Bill Yates shoveled coal, J. B. Lawrence was the passenger conductor, Jay Griffin and Bill Kehle served as brakemen, and J. H. Brown was the baggagemaster.

"We have often heard of the scenery of this canon, but no one can have the faintest conception of its grandeur and magnificence until they have made a trip through it," observed the editor of the Gunnison Review-Press. He thought it was the "largest and most rugged canon in the world traversed by the iron horse," and sat on the roof of one of the cars, the better to see the view.

It is a narrow gorge with walls of granite rising in some places to a height of thousands of feet. On the opposite side are walls still higher, partially covered with a growth of cedar and spruce, with an occasional grove

Cimarron was an important helper engine station between Gunnison and Montrose. Here the line emerged from the Black Canon, and started up the 4% grade of Cerro Summit. The two views at left show the town from the southwest in 1885 and southeast in 1886. In the lower photo there is a passenger train of a baggage, coach, and five Pullmans apparently headed for Gunnison (the locomotive may be behind the engine-house), while two engines and two cars appear to be headed uphill from the water tower. (Upper, John P. Soule, University of Utah; lower, McKee, Denver Public Library Western Coll.) Plenty of little 2-8-0s were needed for the steep Cerro grade when traffic was brisk; here, three Baldwin C-16s (nos. 267, 287, and 260) wait with steam up at the engine-house (above, R. A. Ronzio Collection). Below, a rare 1886 view shows a passenger train stopped on Cerro hill one snowy day; the coach at left is followed by five Pullman cars — curiously, the same consist as in the photo opposite. As the regular "Pacific Express" through limited was scheduled past Cimarron at night, these both may have been specials; in any event, there is an implication of heavy tourist travel on the line in the mid-eighties. (Museum Coll.)

Cimarron, Colorado. 1886. D&RG R.R.

When the D&RG line over Cerro reached the Uncompahgre River, a station was established at Montrose. Even in 1885, Montrose was still little more than a muddy spot in the wide expanse of the Uncompahgre Valley, as indicated by the photos on this page; the unpretentious depot and a half dozen other plain board buildings made up the town. (Top, Museum Coll.; bottom, McKee, Denver Public Library Western Coll.) As the photos opposite reveal, however, in a few years Montrose had become an important narrow gauge junction. At top, tenwheeler 175 waits with the passenger while a small 2-8-0 with a work train trundles past; the coal yard advertises both Crested Butte and Castle Gate (Utah) coal (Denver Public Library Western Coll.). Below, tenwheeler 164 stands at the platform with the through express, while the 83 and another 2-8-0 wait alongside — one, no doubt, with the Ouray train. (Museum Coll.)

Irrigation made the Montrose area important agriculturally. At the dedication of the Gunnison irrigation tunnel in 1909, President Taft rode on the special above — with 4-6-0 no. 168, a coach, and business cars P, B, and N. Below D&RG 400 and 421 pass the project's headquarters and power plant (east of Montrose at Lujave) in July, 1908, with the regular Marshall Pass passenger train. (Both, Museum Coll.)

of quaking aspen. The distance through the canon is fifteen miles. The last mile follows up the Gunnison, and it is said that this last mile has cost more money than the entire work of the grand canon through the Royal Godge of the Arkansas. It is solid cutting the entire distance.

He concluded that it was a "canon that no road but the Denver & Rio Grande would have had the nerve to take hold of."

Kezar and Soap Creek had meanwhile become ghost camps; the latter had only five buildings left, one empty structure and four saloons, although it was rumored that Fry's gang of 300 men would soon move back to Soap Creek to use it as a base from which to push work on the Lake Fork Branch.

The new railhead was Cimarron, a townsite having been laid out on the ranch of W. M. Cline at the upper end of the Cimarron Canon. The railroad wye at the end of track had been laid out on August 12, crossing the stream on two legs. The three hundred men in the track gangs were laying sidings and pushing track up towards Cerro Summit. The bridge builders and surveyors, another 150 men, were preparing to move ahead with their 200 mules and 80 wagons to set up camp twelve miles further west. On the sidings at Cimarron were 27 railroad construction "hotels" or boarding cars, which the *Review Press* commented "give the new town a metropolitan appearance."

Five miles upriver from Cimarron were camped Companies D, H, L, and M of the Ninth (Negro) Cavalry under Major T. W. Dewees, supplied with 14 wagons, two ambulances and a pack train of fifty mules. The battalion was accompanied by an 18 piece band as well as a field trader, so was apparently not expecting any Indian trouble, although its mission was to force the final removal of the Ute Indians to the new reservation in Utah. Nevertheless, the Ute War of 1879 was not so far in the past that the Negro troopers were not a comfort to have close at hand.

On August 25, the last Sanderson stage coaches arrived in Gunnison from Lake City and Ouray. On the

following day, the Lake City stages began operations out of Kezar, while the Montrose and Ouray stages commenced running from Cimarron. Again the railroad was progressively putting the stage lines out of business.

Early in September the Denver Exposition was to take place, and while the D&RG scheduled a special train from Gunnison consisting of "three Palace Coaches and two Chair Cars (equipment unequaled)" with the addition of sleeping cars at Salida, the Denver, South Park & Pacific was spiking its track down towards Gunnison hoping to run a competing special. Both railroads planned to charge $11.50, having agreed between them on the price. The South Park line's advertisement stated it was by "eighty-five miles the shortest route between Gunnison and Denver," noting that it passed through the famous Alpine Tunnel with the "unrivalled scenery on either side of the divide to charm the eye of the traveler . . ."

By Wednesday, August 30, the South Park line looked as if it would make good its promise to be in Gunnison in time to operate the Exposition Special on September 3, for the end of track was at Biebel's ranch three miles from Gunnison, and from the second floors of buildings in town one could see the smoke of the construction engine. The Union Pacific's agent, Henry Ames, wrote the Daily *Review-Press* that the excursion special on the South Park line on September 3 would have a "full compliment of Pullman Day Coaches, rich in finish . . . from which will be afforded a magnificent outlook from the large, full plate glass windows that furnished the tourist with the advantages of an open observation car, minus the accompaniments of dirt and smoke experienced in the last named." This was, of course, a dig at the Rio Grande, which operated such open cars. Gunnison residents thus had their choice of an all day ride through Alpine Tunnel and over Trout Creek and Kenosha Passes, or an overnight trip via Marshall Pass and the Royal Gorge. In the September 1 issue of the newspaper, ads of the competing roads were run in the same column on page 4.

At noon on Saturday, September 2, 1882, the tracklayers of the Denver, South Park & Pacific reached the rails of the D&RG's Crested Butte branch, which they had to cross to connect with the empty new stone roundhouse which had so long awaited their coming The Union Pacific subsidiary had arrived just in the nick of time to prepare for their Sunday excursion special. It had taken the South Park company nearly thirteen months longer than the D&RG to reach Gunnison, a consequence of the disastrous mistake of drilling Alpine Tunnel.

On September 3, in preparation for "Gunnison Day" at the exposition in Denver, both roads ran passenger-packed specials. The South Park train pulled out shortly after 6 a.m. with six coach loads and engines and cars decorated with flags. At 12:40 the Denver & Rio Grande special headed east with seven coach loads, a total of more than 200 passengers, including many from Crested Butte, Irwin, Tin Cup and other camps in the region. Later, regular trains on both roads carried additional passengers to Denver, and between 500 and 800 residents of the Gunnison region were estimated to have gone to the fair. To cap it off, a ceremony for the South Park road was held in Gunnison on September 5, and it was "right joyously welcomed," which no doubt meant that booze flowed. In fact, the west end of town was draped in flags, a bon-fire was built in the street, a temporary outdoor bar dispensed free beer, and cigars were handed out readily. "One railroad is a good thing," intoned a pompous speaker from a makeshift platform erected in the street, "but two roads are better. The one holds the other in check." The advent of the South Park line, he predicted, would force D&RG freight rates down. He overlooked the fact that the two roads had already shown a desire to avoid a rate war; and he overlooked the fact that the South Park had proved more expensive to build than the Marshall Pass line of the D&RG, a fact not at all conducive to low rates.

Meanwhile the Denver & Rio Grande railhead was creeping over

Cedar Creek (Cerro) Summit towards Montrose. Beyond Montrose, graders had already finished the line to Kahnah Creek. Fifteen more miles of difficult grading from Kahnah Creek to Grand Junction would complete the heavy work that far, and those fifteen miles were in the capable hands of Orman, Crook & Company, who faced some troublesome rock work in the lower Gunnison Canon.

From Grand Junction west to the Utah border lay another stretch of grade contracted out to Hammond & Hendricks, and the fifteen miles down the Grand (Colorado) River Valley were nearly completed by September 2, 1882. At that point the grade would leave the river to cross the badlands below the Book Cliffs, and the contractors were having water wagons built at the shop of J. L. Robinson in Grand Junction to enable them to haul water for the desert grading.

These contractors were also completing the grading of the Grand Junction yards, located in eighty acres of depot land owned by the railroad. As usual, the railroad was a partner in the town company, half-owner in this case. Grand Junction was already a growing place. The townsite had been selected as early as September 26, 1881, surveyed in January, 1882, and the town incorporated in July, but the real boom was just now beginning as the railroad approached. A two-story brick hotel was going up, a town company office was under construction, and three brick yards were in full operation to supply the construction boom. The clay obtainable nearby was reported equal to the product mined near Golden. "The town has had its period of log houses, next 'adobe' and now has reached the 'golden age' of 'brick'," commented one newspaper.

Another town that sprang up ahead of the railroad was Montrose. Located seven miles below the military post called Cantonment Uncompahgre on the Uncompahgre River, a tributary of the Gunnison, Montrose had been located on January 20, 1882, and laid out with streets and avenues 100 feet wide. The first building was already there,

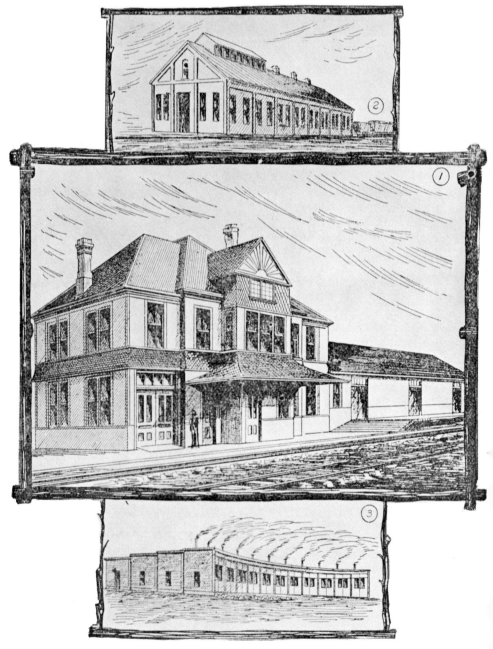

When no. 83, the "Sierra La Sal," entered Grand Junction for the first time on Nov. 21, 1882, the town was already thriving, and the D&RG promptly erected imposing shops, depot, and roundhouse (opposite). By 1884 the town looked busy and prosperous in the photos below, all taken around Main Street. In the second photo the D&RG facilities can be seen in the distance. (Top left, Museum Coll.; others, Grand Junction Sentinel.)

a frame structure having been put up by one John Baird on January 1. Subsequent structures were less elegant; a number of log and picket houses were erected in February. In April, however, W. A. Eckerly & Company established a sawmill 14 miles southwest of town, and frame buildings proliferated thereafter, including a bank, newspaper, stage barn, and several stores. The town was incorporated in April, town officers were elected in May, and by July there were about 125 houses in Montrose.

Slowly the track layers approached the new townsite, and on September 8, 1882, it having taken a month to lay the 24 miles of rail westward from Cimarron, the "front" reached Montrose.

Construction of track from Montrose to Delta went more quickly; the trackbuilders did not have the curves and grades of the Squaw Hills to deal with, as they had over Cedar Creek Summit, for the country beyond Montrose was relatively level. They laid track into Delta on September 22, 1882. Delta was of course the product of another of these town companies in which the railway owned half interest.

The first issue of the Grand Junction *News* on October 28 reported that a thousand men were at work on the final grading in the lower canyon of the Gunnison below Delta: "The cannonade of the blasting is heard day and night." In the grading camp a mile and a quarter south of Grand Junction near the end of October Michael Shillaney and J. C. Johnson tried a shortcut to opening a keg of powder by using a pick; they struck a spark and the keg exploded, burning them badly. Cutting through rock meant blasting, and the use of explosives always seemed to involve accidents due to haste, ignorance or carelessness.

Tracklayers by October 28 were twenty miles northwest of Delta, approaching Bridgeport in the canyon. The November 4 newspaper noted that "The D&RG managers are pushing the work on their road very rapidly, and we may soon expect the little 'iron horse' to come puffing and snorting into Grand Junction bringing with it thousands

57

Even after standard gauging, Grand Junction remained an important narrow gauge terminal. Above, tenwheeler no. 164 stands at the Grand Junction depot with the Marshall Pass express, amid a scene of typical depot platform activity and inactivity (in the case of the gents in the shadows at right). Below, the dual-gauge Grand Junction yards are spread out beneath us, with the roundhouse and shops at left, depot distant center, and ice house at right. Even at this late date, narrow gauge engines predominate. (Both Grand Junction Sentinel.) At right, the yards layout as it appeared by 1890 (John Buvinger).

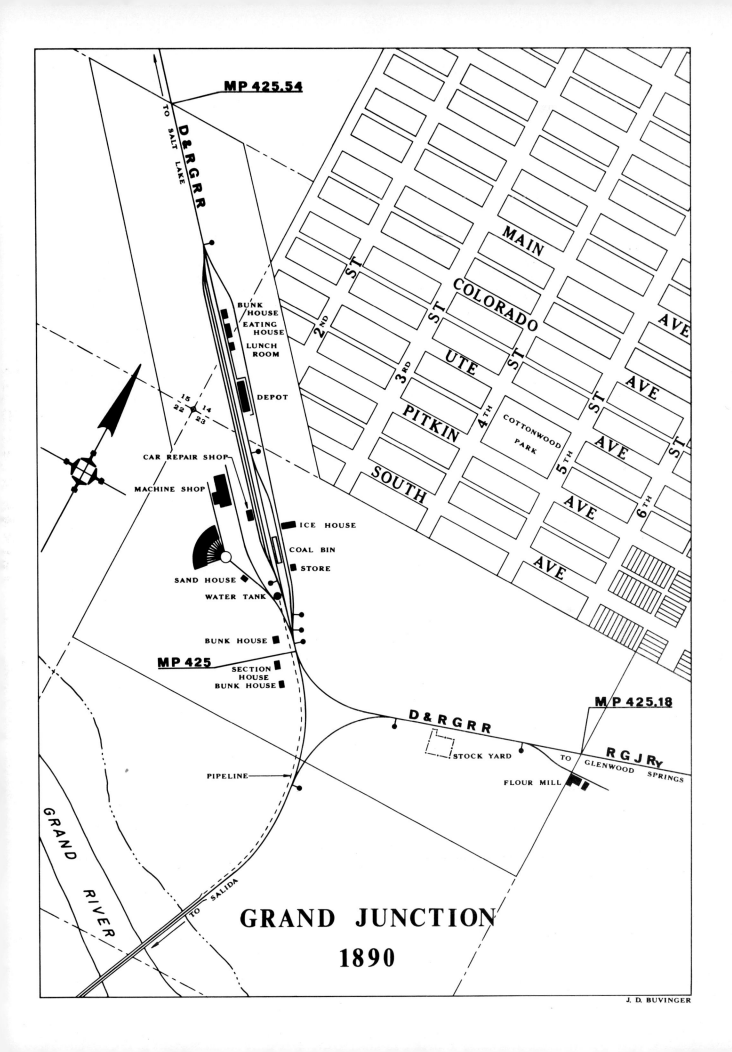

MP 425.54

TO SALT LAKE

D & R G R R

BUNK HOUSE
EATING HOUSE
LUNCH ROOM
DEPOT

15 14
22 23

CAR REPAIR SHOP

MACHINE SHOP

ICE HOUSE
COAL BIN
STORE

SAND HOUSE
WATER TANK

BUNK HOUSE

MP 425

SECTION HOUSE
BUNK HOUSE

PIPELINE

TO SALIDA

MAIN

COLORADO

AVE

2ND ST

3RD ST

UTE

ST

AVE

PITKIN

4TH ST

COTTONWOOD PARK

5TH ST

AVE

ST

SOUTH

AVE

6TH ST

AVE

MP 425.18

D & R G R R

STOCK YARD

R G J Ry

TO GLENWOOD SPRINGS

FLOUR MILL

GRAND RIVER

GRAND JUNCTION
1890

J. D. BUVINGER

After initial construction the line was frequently upgraded. A new bridge was installed over the Colorado at Grand Junction in 1904; one of the first narrow gauge trains across it (above) had a typical consist — tenwheeler, a pair of baggage and mail cars, two coaches, and a parlor car (Utah State Hist. Society Coll.). A long tunnel was put in at Bridgeport to avoid a circuitous route off to the left. The only tunnel on the D&RG narrow gauge except for those at Toltec, it is still in use for standard gauge (right, R. W. Richardson photo).

of people to populate our beautiful valley . . ." Twelve heavy freight wagons had passed through town the previous Monday with supplies for the railroad builders. The town was growing so fast that tents were being put up for use as lodging houses. "A great improvement on nothing," commented the Grand Junction *News* sourly.

On November 9, a bridge gang began construction of a truss bridge over the Grand River at Grand Junction. "It will be the longest and largest bridge on the Utah Extension of the D&RG Railway," noted the *News*. The railway's resident engineer had meanwhile moved his headquarters into Grand Junction to be near the approaching railhead.

The company suffered a minor setback on November 19 when a work train piled up near Whitewater. The engine, towing a string of empty supply cars, was backing down towards Delta when it hit a rock and derailed, seven cars piling up after it and injuring one man seriously. But the mishap did not halt tracklaying, which continued at a rate of three and a half or four miles per day.

Grand Junction continued to grow; it had even acquired its first Chinese resident, an important enough occurence for the newspaper to interview the gentleman. Mr. Yup Mow had moved there to open a laundry, having run one for quite some time in Gunnison. The *News* commented that he had "great faith in Grand Junction."

Shortly before 4 p.m. on Tuesday, November 21, 1882, Rio Grande tracklayers completed laying rails over the Grand River bridge, which had just been finished. A party of men and women from Grand Junction walked over the bridge to board the first train to cross into the town. At 4:50 p.m. the engineer whistled, hauled back on the throttle, and at exactly 4:53 Engine 83, the *Sierra La Sal*, rolled slowly over the Colorado River. "LINKED AT LAST," proclaimed the subsequent issue of the *News*: "This morning the iron horse 'paweth in the valley'," a Grand Junction resident wrote a friend in Denver. On Thursday, November 24, the first through

freight arrived, and a special train brought Division Superintendent J. C. Meyers into town.

The usual construction of railroad servicing facilities followed. Rock for the foundation of the freight depot and water tank was on the ground by December 2 and the tank was nearing completion by December 16. The November 25 issue of the *News* reported that track layers were laying three and a half to four miles per day down the level floor of the Grand Valley on the grade completed some months before. On December 19 it was completed 25.6 miles to the border between Utah and Colorado, as far as the Denver & Rio Grande company could build on its own behalf.

Grand Junction, meanwhile, was rapidly assuming the appearance and atmosphere of a railroad town. General Manager Dodge arrived in his private train and as usual spoke highly of the new town to its citizens; after all, his company owned half interest in the town. On December 15 the first regular rail postal car arrived. The photographer William Henry Jackson came and took some photographs of the town, as he had just done in the Black Canon. Excursions arrived from Montrose and Leadville.

The prospect of railroad transportation in this region even interested the United States Army, whose military post up north on the White River near the site of the Meeker Massacre of 1879 was supplied from Rawlins on the Union Pacific 150 miles away. The army scout Luther "Yellowstone" Kelly arrived in Grand Junction just before Christmas in the process of looking for a route for a military road between the town and the White River post.

By January 20, 1883, timber for the freight depot was on the ground, and the railroad was making preparations to erect a sturdier iron bridge on stone piers to replace the wooden structure over the Grand River. One of the large wooden trusses had already been damaged by ice floating down the stream, and more would come towards spring.

D. C. Dodge arrived again in the middle of January and immediately headed for the telegraph operator

in order to dispatch a fistful of telegrams. He told the newspaper editor that Grand Junction would be made a division terminus, and that the company would erect a roundhouse and machine shops. This of course meant a permanent force of railway employees resident in Grand Junction, an important economic boost for the town. Material was soon shipped in for a two-story "Queen Anne" style passenger depot, and an eight stall roundhouse and turntable were begun. (The roundhouse eventually had eleven stalls.) Grand Junction was indeed well on the way to becoming a railroad town.

Construction in Utah

Building the western end of his great railroad system faced William Jackson Palmer with a problem in corporate organization, for the Denver & Rio Grande Railway was not incorporated to build or operate trackage in the Territory of Utah. The obvious answer was to incorporate a Utah company to perform this task — and in fact a number of companies became involved. Palmer's agent, Dr. William Bell, commenced by organizing the first of these companies, the Sevier Valley Railway, on December 7, 1880, to build from Ogden to the northern border of Arizona, via Salt Lake City, through Provo and Spanish Fork Canon to Salina in the Sevier Valley, then to the northern border of Arizona. (Another company, the Arizona Northern Railway, was incorporated in Arizona to connect with the Sevier Valley Railway at the border, with a projected crossing of the Colorado River at Lee's Ferry.)

A second route of the Sevier Valley Railway was to extend from Salina east through Salina Pass, across the Castle Valley and Buckhorn Flat — there were in fact a variety of possible routes in this region — to a crossing of the Green River near the 39th Parallel, then eastward to the Colorado border, where it would connect with the Denver & Rio Grande Railway west of Grand Junction. No thought was at this time given to crossing Soldier Pass on a more direct route, probably because Palmer, blocked by the Tripartite Agreement from building south of Espanola, was *still* thinking in terms of a north-south line. If he could not build from Denver to Mexico City he would build from Ogden to Mexico City via Arizona. After all, he still controlled the narrow gauge Mexican National Railway. In this frame of reference, the reluctance of the D&RG management to cross the Wasatch farther north than Salina Pass is easily explicable; while perhaps nearer in terms of time to accomplishment, and while a source of revenue in the immediate future, the east-west connection with Colorado may in fact have been secondary in their minds to the north-south line into Arizona, with the latter assuming geographical pre-eminence and the question of the point of connection with the Colorado line of secondary importance. Furthermore, Price River Canon, the logical eastern approach to Soldier Pass, was reputed to be a very treacherous canon indeed. Finally, much of the country in central Utah was very sketchily known, and without further exploration Salina Pass may have seemed to be the best answer.

At the time this work had begun, the Utah Central standard gauge railroad extended from Ogden through Salt Lake City to Provo, and a narrow gauge road known as the Utah & Pleasant Valley Railway crossed the Wasatch Range by using Spanish Fork Canon, Clear Creek Canon and a switchback line over the range south of Soldier Pas. This did not seem at the time particularly significant to the organizers of the Sevier Valley Railway.

Since the key point in railroad strategy in central Utah seemed to be Salina Pass, Chief Engineer M. T. Burgess set up headquarters in the town of Salina. On December 8, 1880, the day following incorporation of the Sevier Valley company, he sent a location party to occupy the western approach to Salina Pass preparatory to obtaining legal title to that route. On December 12, the surveyors began running a transit line west from Salina Summit, and by December 22, had completed 14 miles of location.

Another two locating parties, better equipped, had left Salt Lake City on December 16, one headed for Salina Pass, the other for the crossing of the Colorado River near Lee's Ferry. But a week later Burgess learned that the Utah Southern Railroad was planning to dispute the Sevier Valley Railway's occupation of Salina Pass, so he sent out a message diverting the Lee's Ferry survey to speed work east of Salina.

On Christmas Day Burgess personally located part of the line in the strategic narrows six miles east of Salina known as Rattlesnake Point, and with assistance from his preliminary survey party, began token construction of the roadbed. This was the first actual construction undertaken in the interest of the Denver & Rio Grande in Utah. Ironically, rails were never laid there.

On the following day, December 26, the two parties from Salt Lake finally arrived in Salina, augmenting Burgess' forces, and the chief engineer adopted the strategy of occupying those points over Salina Pass, especially on its western canon approaches, that were too narrow to accommodate more than one railroad. The surveying party under Assistant Engineer F. M. Wilbor went to work to complete the location at Rattlesnake Point. The second party from Salt Lake under Assistant Engineer R. E. Ball located detached pieces of line at the Alum Beds and the Saw Tooth Narrows. The result of this work was four disconnected segments of location, surveyed without relation to one another and at different levels, in order to perfect legal title by prior occupation. Ball finally proceeded to connect the various segments, work which he completed on February 13, 1881. Having secured first occupation at all strategic points prior to the Utah Southern, that company withdrew its engineers, leaving the Sevier Valley Railway in undisputed possession of the western approaches to Salina Pass. Subsequent surveying completed a line down the eastern side.

The ensuing history of Rio Grande enterprise in Utah was almost as complicated as that in Colorado. As in Colorado, company surveyors ranged far and wide, exploring vast reaches of western, central, southern, and eastern Utah. Much of this was desert country, much of it comparatively unknown. Just as in Colorado, only a small percentage of the mileage surveyed ever had track laid on it, and just as in Colorado, miles of grade were built, as at Salina Pass, never to be used. As in Colorado, the company in Utah found it necessary to beat other competing railroads to strategic routes where canyon passages were so narrow that only one line of rails could be laid.

On May 25, 1881, Palmer's Utah associates incorporated the Salt Lake and Park City Railway Company to build a short feeder line to the Coalville Mines. But the most important step taken by Palmer was the incorporation on July 21, 1881, of the *Denver & Rio Grande Western Railway Company*, (not to be confused with the 20th Century D&RGW Rail*road*), embracing a vast number of projected routes, and immediately consolidating under the new corporate title the two companies organized earlier.

The new D&RGW Railway quickly absorbed three small 3′ gauge mining roads south of Salt Lake City—the Bingham Canon & Camp Floyd, from Sandy (in the Jordan River valley) west to the Bingham copper district; the Wasatch & Jordan Valley, from Sandy east to Alta and the Little Cottonwood mining district; and the Utah & Pleasant Valley, from Provo to the Pleasant Valley coal mines (south of Soldier Summit). The first two had been begun in 1872 as separate independent lines, but subsequently fell under the control of a New Yorker named C. W. Scofield. Scofield then acquired the struggling and uncompleted U&PV, pushing the tracks on to the coal fields, and from Springville into Provo, in 1879. The three-road combine was overextended financially, however, and the two smaller roads could not support the unsuccessful U&PV. Failure to pay bond interest in 1881 brought foreclosure and sale of the BC&CF to the D&RGW in September and the W&JV in December. The U&PV was not acquired until the next summer; William S. Spackman, treasurer of the Denver & Rio Grande Western, bid in for the little road at a foreclosure sale on June 14 at Provo. The little lines provided a nucleus for the projected D&RGW operations, as well as nine small Porter, Dawson Baily and Baldwin locomotives of varied vintage and a quantity of rolling stock. Other equipment for the early D&RGW operations had to be brought over from Denver on standard gauge flat cars via the Union Pacific and its subsidiary Utah Central.

But this is getting ahead of the story. To go back a year, 1881, in addition to encompassing the incorporation of the D&RGW and its absorption of narrow gauge feeder lines, was a year of exploring and surveying. Chief Engineer Burgess at first had his men working on lines east of Salina Pass. His surveyors ran lines from the base of the pass north to Castle Valley Junction (Price) and east to Green River, over a variety of routes. But none of these was destined to be built.

The clearest way to unravel the tangle of surveys is to examine the route that actually became the main line, taking it in geographical sequence. The first important segment was that from Salt Lake City to the mouth of Spanish Fork Canon. This was a stated objective of both the Denver & Rio Grande Western Railway and its predecessor Sevier Valley company. The line was paralleled along its entire route by the existing standard gauge UP subsidiary, the Utah Central, which connected Salt Lake and Provo.

Both the UC and the projected D&RGW narrow gauge line followed the eastern edge of the Jordan River Valley, the river being a stream which flows from Utah Lake north into the Great Salt Lake west of Salt Lake City. All of the Jordan Valley was once beneath an inland sea, and when the sea receded it left a bench of land extending out from the mountain ranges east and west of the valley. When the ancient inland sea slowly dried up, Utah Lake separated from the Great Salt Lake, leaving between the two a narrow piece of this benchland which extended clear across the valley like a dyke. However, in flowing from Utah Lake north to the Great Salt Lake, the Jordan River had over the eons cut a brief little canyon only three miles long through this benchland. The Utah Central line had not employed this canyon, known as the Jordan Narrows, but climbed over the benchland which was several hundred feet higher, some distance east of the river, using a grade of sixty feet to the mile.

In the spring of 1881, Sevier Valley Railway officials learned that the Utah Central company contemplated changing its line from the high location to the canyon in order to eliminate the grade, also to shorten their line by 2½ miles. Immediately a Sevier Valley engineering party set out from Salt Lake and on April 5, 1881, occupied the Jordan Narrows by beginning to locate and grade a line through them. "The Narrows were the key to the Division," Chief Engineer Burgess later reported. The location for the entire line was completed on September 28. Grading contracts for that whole division were awarded between October 24 and November 1, 1881, and grading commenced about November 1. By the end of the year—which was a mere sixty days—ninety percent of the roadbed was graded and rail had been laid for seven miles south of Salt Lake City. The right-of-way map for those portions of the line that were on public land was approved by the Secretary of the Interior on November 26, 1881, but most of the line was through private lands, which had to be obtained either

The first oasis reached by the narrow gauge line running west from the Colorado border was Green River — a rough little frontier town established at the point where the tracks crossed the Green, a major tributary of the Colorado. A fine hotel, with tree shaded lawns, was quickly built beside the tracks; it was initially called the "Palmer House". (State Historical Society of Colorado.)

through negotiated purchase or, in the case of reluctant landowners, condemnation. Eight condemnation suits were necessary.

Lumbermen were meanwhile cutting trees for ties and bridge or culvert timber in Spanish Fork Canon. The company could obtain natural ballast at the head of the Jordan Narrows, and they anticipated obtaining coal with which to fuel engines from the Pleasant Valley coal mines via the Utah & Pleasant Valley narrow gauge. On June 14, 1882, Rio Grande Western Construction Company track crews — this firm being a Palmer subsidiary organized to build the D&RGW Railway—laid track into the outskirts of Provo.

Three little narrow gauge lines were absorbed by the new D&RG Ry.; all were mining roads. At right, a small gondola of the Wasatch & Jordan Valley RR is hand loaded with ore sometime in the seventies (Coll. of LDS Church Historian's Office). The Utah & Pleasant Valley had been built to serve the Pleasant Valley coal fields south of Provo. At top opposite, a construction crew pauses during the laying of track in Pleasant Valley; while in the bottom photo opposite D&RGW 2-8-0 no. 77 waits at the Scofield depot in the late eighties with a train of northbound coal. The contemporary photo, below, of no. 74 is typical of the power received by the Western from the parent D&RG. (Three photos, Utah State Historical Society.)

One of the first trains into town was a special that brought D&RGW Treasurer Spackman and the party of officials that purchased the Utah & Pleasant Valley line that very day. By that evening, when they left to return to Salt Lake City, the D&RGW track was laid to the depot of the U&PV. By the stroke of a pen that day and by the connection of track between the two narrow gauge lines, the D&RGW was extended 38 miles up towards Soldier Pass in the Wasatch (and in fact it extended on over the range by a different pass to the Pleasant Valley).

It was clear from the very beginning that although the U&PV crossed the main range of the Wasatch, which is precisely what the D&RGW would have to do, possession of the Utah & Pleasant Valley line did not solve the Western's problem. D&RGW engineers had made track surveys of the U&PV in the fall of 1881, before the purchase, and Chief Engineer Burgess concluded that in the building of that line, considerations of grade, alignment, roadbed, structures, and the cost of operation had all been sacrificed to economy in construction. The crossing of the Wasatch above Clear Creek was accomplished with the aid of grades exceeding 4.5 per cent as well as switchbacks, which no railway that hoped to remain solvent could consider employing for main line operation. "It is a costly and uncertain line to operate," Burgess wrote Weitbrec early in 1882. "I could not recommend its permanent use even as a coal spur," he added; "Ultimately this portion of the track should be torn up and relaid down Fish Creek (a stream east of the Wasatch) . . ."

To trace the steps that led to the selection of a route over Soldier Summit, the next segment of D&RGW main line east of the U&PV at Clear Creek, one must again go back in time to early 1881 when Burgess was headquartered at Salina. About January 26 that year, the chief engineer was told by the management to survey a line north from the eastern base of Salina Pass to a junction with the Utah & Pleasant Valley *east* of the Wasatch, and he assigned Assistant Engineer Wil-

bor to that task. The management was still thinking of Salina Pass as the point at which the Rio Grande line would cross the mountains, and apparently wanted a connection there with the source of coal in Pleasant Valley.

However in February, 1881, D&RG Chief Engineer McMurtrie had sent the able and experienced engineer Fred Mathyas, who had recently located part of the Albuquerque Extension, to survey the Utah situation and render his opinion. Mathyas proceeded to explore westward from Gunnison down that river to its confluence with the Grand River (where Grand Junction would be built), and he then rode westward, examining the country along the base of the Book Cliffs to the Green River crossing. From Green River he worked due west across Buckhorn Flat to the Castle Valley at the eastern base of Salina Pass. In March, Mathyas arrived in the town of Salina and presented Burgess with his reports. Another of McMurtrie's engineers, M. F. Hurd, followed Mathyas' route, but presented reports much less optimistic regarding grade and curvature.

During March, meanwhile, Burgess sent Mathyas to examine the eastern side of Salina Pass working north to the Cottonwood and Huntingdon drainages, and while doing this work the Colorado engineer completed the first thorough reconnoissance of the Upper Price River Canon and Soldier Pass, still with an eye to a connection from Salina Pass to the U&PV east of the range. Another of Burgess' engineers had pointed out that the Price River canon was nowhere as formidable as had been assumed, and Mathyas confirmed this. But it was Mathyas himself who was apparently the first man to suggest a line crossing Soldier Pass to connect with the U&PV at Clear Creek. If his suggestion were followed, it would, together with a connection down Fish Creek to the Pleasant Valley on the east side of the range, eliminate the U&PV switchback line, and more important, it would eliminate the necessity of crossing Salina Pass as far as a connection eastward to Colorado was concerned.

D&RGW surveyors ran a prelim-

inary line over Soldier Summit in April, 1881, and in July and August a line with 3.5 per cent and some 4 per cent grades was completed from Clear Creek to the summit. Later this was resurveyed to a line with maximum grades of 3.8 per cent and maximum curves of 16 degrees. Grading contracts for this line were let in April, even before the final survey was begun.

Location eastward from Soldier Summit had also begun in April, as had location westward from Dead Horse Crossing at the eastern base of the pass. The two parties met in Upper Price Canon on June 19, 1881, having completed a line which ran through the spectacular rock formations at Castle Gate. Thus by the middle of 1881 the Western had a line surveyed over the Wasatch to the desert east of Price, and the line running from Salina Pass directly eastward over Buckhorn Flat to the Green River Crossing remained on paper.

The last portion of the line to be surveyed was that from the upper Price River canon to Green River and on to the Colorado border, despite the preliminary examinations made by Mathyas and Hurd in the spring of 1881. The country was mostly desert, the type of terrain called by the early French fur trappers in the region *mauve terre* and by the Spanish explorers *mal pais*—both terms translated into English as "bad lands." To the north, the impressive and forbidding Roan Cliffs and Book Cliffs stretched for more than a hundred miles in a great east-west arc. The railway had to cross a nearly barren blue shale mesa region below these cliffs that was cut by a vast number of ravines draining from the Book Cliffs southwest to the Green River and south and southeast to the Grand (Colorado) River. Cutting at right angles across these drainages, the track would have to cross one dry wash after another, each capable of spawning flash floods in the summer. Between the major drainages, the track would have to surmount one summit after another, with numerous up and down grades that stretched the distance the rails would have to negotiate. The main divide between the Green and Grand

Rivers would be crossed a mile south of the Book Cliffs at an altitude of 5,153 feet, 1,084 feet higher than the Green River crossing.

As mentioned earlier, Mathyas and Hurd had both examined this area and come to different conclusions. Mathyas, according to the Western's chief engineer, was "misled" in respect to the height of ridges between drainages. "The country does not admit of the easy grade and cheap line promised by the exploring engineer's report," concluded Burgess. Major Hurd seemed to be closer to the mark.

The first D&RGW locating party crossed the Green River from the west early in May, 1881, and started a preliminary line eastward, which they ran clear to a point on the Gunnison River in Colorado. (They also ran a branch as far as the mouth of the Dolores River.) Between the Green River and the Colorado border they discovered that the line would have to cross not only the main divide between the Green and the Grand, but seven principal drainages such as Saleratus Wash, Cottonwood and Westwater Creeks which led south from the Book Cliffs, not to mention the myriad dry washes tributary to the major drainages. East of the Colorado border the line would have to cross the divide between Bitter Water and Salt Creek, and another divide between Salt Creek and the the Grand River Valley. The names of these desert water courses (often only dry washes) were indicative of a major trouble the railroad would face — not only the extremes of flash floods or a shortage of water, but bad water when it was present, impregnated with alkali and other chemical impurities that rendered it unfit for use in locomotive boilers.

Around August 1, 1881, Western survey parties commenced extensive final surveys to lay out a roadbed with a one per cent maximum grade, the result being a line 88.5 miles long from Green River to the border. The curves were to be a maximum of ten degrees. The engineers anticipated little difficulty in grading, for although shale was found within two feet of the surface throughout most of the badlands, the soil being shallow and generally

barren, even the shale was much less difficult to excavate than solid rock. However, because of the presence of shale so near the surface, pile trestles often could not be employed. Since the country was susceptable to flash flooding, Burgess concluded that "an unusual amount of open drainage" would be necessary for the safety of the line. "Box culverts are seldom advisable," he told his superiors. Where pile trestles and box culverts could not be used, the Western was thus forced to build the impressive stone culverts to support its fills that remain in that desert today.

By June 14, 1882, the D&RGW had laid fifty miles of track to Provo, and that same day added to the system the 56.4 miles of the Utah & Pleasant Valley Railroad, although only the 38 miles from Provo to Clear Creek was of any use, and then only with heavy upgrading and rebuilding. By August 1, the company had completed another 14.4 miles of track eastward from Clear Creek over Soldier Pass and down the east side to Fish Creek.

On that date, August 1, 1882, the Denver & Rio Grande Western Railway in its entirety was leased to the Denver & Rio Grande Railway for completion of construction and operation. The first step of the allied companies was to construct a new line down Fish Creek for 13 miles to intersect the old U&PV trackage about two and a half miles north of Scofield in the Pleasant Valley. Completed and put into operation on December 1, 1882, the new line permitted the scrapping of the torturous switchback line over the Wasatch. Even before this was completed, construction continued eastward down through Castle Gate. The tracklayers reached Price Canon by October 28, 1882, and the first passenger train rolled into Farnham, ten miles beyond Price, on the evening of November 12. Slowly the railhead advanced across the broken desert country towards the Green.

In March, 1883, the *Deseret News* of Salt Lake City published the account of a tourist who had ridden much of the line. His train had pulled out of Salt Lake at 7:40 a.m.,

running southward through the Jordan Narrows, around the northern shore of Utah Lake and through Provo up into Spanish Fork Canon en route to the Castle Valley. It was beyond Clear Creek, where the railroad had a three-stall engine house for helper locomotives, that he found the trip most impressive:

At Clear Creek station the ascent commences to be quite difficult and continues so to the summit (Soldier Summit); from the latter point, however, the train glides over the smooth steel rails to Pleasant Valley Junction (where the new line to Scofield departed from the main line) where we arrived at five p.m., and were hospitably entertained by Mrs. Southworth, former landlady of the Lake Point Hotel. At this station, the last opened for regular travel, we boarded a lumber car on the "construction train" and sped round the point of the mountain where Fish Creek and White River join to form Price River. Along the sinuous banks of the latter, the long train of cars, having loaded with ties, dashed by the tie companys (sic) and saw mills in the canyon at fearful speed. The road is so crooked that Horseshoe Curves are frequent, and we found it quite interesting to keep track of the North Star, appearing first on one side of the car and then the other with such rapidity as to be bewildering to the star gazer. The scenery in the Price River Canyon is very beautiful, reaching its highest attraction at Castle Gate. The latter is the opening made by the stream through a wall of rugged rock rising on one side like a slender promontory reaching into the sky. This promontory extends from the mountain down to the roadside where it is cleanly cut from base to summit, 500 feet above, appearing like a thin slab of red sandstone set on edge.

At Price, which the railroad was calling "Castle Valley Junction" presumably because of the connection with the Salina Pass line that would never be built, the passengers were met and entertained by local officials, who had organized a townsite there expecting the railroad to build a roundhouse and perhaps

Castle Gate is a rift in a high wall of rock that cuts across Price River Canon in central Utah. A rugged and spectacular area, it quickly became a major tourist attraction for the D&RGW. In the rare glass plate view at left, a construction train is pictured at Castle Gate during building of the line. An enlargement of the portion of the photo showing the yards is below left; the construction train of four W&JV flats is being pushed by one of the little ex-Utah & Pleasant Valley engines, probably a Porter 0-6-0 of either U&PV or Bingham Canon & Camp Floyd origin. (C. W. Carter photo, LDS Church Information Office Coll.) The same view is seen from further up the tracks at right (John P. Soule photo, Univ. of Utah Coll.). A similar view taken after standard gauging, below, shows clearly how the new standard gauge track was constructed parallel to the old narrow gauge line, leaving only grade, bridge abutments, and some ties. (Brigham Young Univ. Coll.)

some shops. But the railroad chose to erect bases for "helper" locomotives assigned to boost trains up over Soldier Pass somewhat nearer the base of the pass than Price. On the west side there was a three-stall frame engine house at Clear Creek, where the now-abandoned U&PV line had headed south. East of Soldier Summit the D&RGW had a two-stall engine house at Pleasant Valley Junction which in 1883 was expanded to eleven stalls, built of brick.

Eastward from Price, the tracklayers continued their work across the broken desert country towards the Green River. It was three months earlier, in December 1882, that D&RG tracklayers completed their line to the border west of Grand Junction. The logical thing to do was for them to continue working westward until they met the crews working eastward from Price. Having completed the track to the Utah Line on December 19, the following day they began to lay track in Utah. Their labor and material were charged to the D&RGW, thus avoiding the problem caused by the inability of the D&RG to legally operate in Utah.

By December 23 the line was completed 2.4 miles west of the line to Acheron. On January 8 it was laid to Westwater, 12.8 miles from Colorado. The Grand Junction *News* of January 13 noted that "quite a number of saloons are moving down to the end of the r. r. track," no doubt to alleviate the drouth encountered in the Utah badlands below the Book Cliffs. One stretch of track in this region was a tangent nearly ten miles long, on which track laying must have progressed rapidly. The ties used were hand-hewn Colorado cedar. By January 14 the line was at Cottonwood, 18.6 miles beyond the border, and the tracklayers reached Cisco on February 2, 1883.

On January 27, 1883, the Grand Junction *News* reported that the railroad company was having considerable difficulty with their locomotives at the "front" due to the bad water. "To get good water they have to run back to within twelve or fifteen miles of this place," claimed the *News*. This alkali-impregnated

desert water would continue to plague the narrow gauge line after its completion, as one engineer who worked on the line recalled:

> We used to leave Grand Junction with poor water as a starter, and before we had crossed the desert we exhausted our entire supply of adjectives in attempting to describe it. It was something like this: Poor, very poor, bad, more bad, worse, terrible, fierce, and at Farnham the limit.

The water at Farnham, 1.7 miles east of Price, was so bad, on top of all the other bad water fed into westbound engines, that frequently an engine had to be "killed" at about that location.

> One or more dead engines in almost every west-bound train could be seen in the vicinity of Price at that time . . . We certainly used to resort to all known schemes to stop the leaks and get our engines into town. We would feed her bran, and torn shreads of paper, as well as trying another formula, that many of you know.

One may speculate on the particular additive with which D&RGW engineers tried to doctor their water; it is known that sheep manure was sometimes used on the D&RG.

On February 15 the rails were spiked down into White House, 38 miles west of the border. Five days later, Governor J. B. Grant paid the "front" a visit. Arriving in Grand Junction at 8 p.m. on February 20 in a special train on which D. C. Dodge was a passenger, the Governor was received by a reception committee of local bigwigs who met him in the drawing room of his private car. He then stepped down from the train and walked through double lines of the Grand Valley Guards (otherwise known as Company F of the Colorado National Guard). On the following day, Wednesday, the governor accompanied General Manager Dodge and Superintendent Meyers out to the end of track in Utah.

The railroad crossing of the Green River lay between the approaching railheads, and a settlement had naturally developed at that point. Dr. Stroud of Grand Junction who visited Green River about this time thought the settlement had some

future possibilities for farming and grazing, but that they were not yet realized. "Just at present the Doctor thinks it is the headquarters of Hell," reported the Grand Junction *News*: "Grand Junction on the one hand and Salt Lake City on the other, being the nearest points where the majesty of the law is recognized, there have naturally collected at Green River the worst elements of creation."

The doctor's business in Green River settlement had been created by one of these "worst elements," whom the doctor characterized as the "Green River Dancing Master," a fellow with a most unusual manner of teaching:

> When he had secured a pupil, his style was to draw a couple of revolvers and beat time with them; at every beat a bullet went through the place where one foot was placed, or through the foot, in case the owner did not take care of it. This naturally produced an alternate motion of the feet, and when the beat was rapid enough a very vigorous style of dancing resulted. When unusually full of old "forty rod" said dancing master crossed the river and entered a saloon, and proceeded to organize a class; but the class held him down, and he concluded to postpone the lesson. Going to the bar he called for an "eye-opener" and laid his revolver, ready cocked, on the counter. As the bar-tender turned around he presented too good a mark to be missed, and the gentleman . . . pulled the trigger and sent a bullet through the fellow's lungs. The crowd followed (the assailant) to the street and all blazed away at him. One bullet struck him in the leg, and moved by his groans, the crowd picked him up tenderly, carried him back, and to ease his pain, gave him *three ounces* of laudanum (a lethal dose of pain-killer). It eased him. They didn't have to call him out to a telegraph pole, as they had intended.

The doctor had been called to attend the bar-tender; at least the latter was still alive when Stroud rode back to the end of track to take a train on into Grand Junction.

An ex-D&RG Baldwin 2-8-0 poses at the East Portal of Castle Gate with an early Western narrow gauge freight. (Alex Martin photo, author's collection.)

At left, the spire at Castle Gate can be seen from the south (top) and west. The south view in particular provides a good comparison of relative size; the large water tower is dwarfed by the huge pillar of rock, and the crew working on the track and little Porter engine pushing the work train are almost indistinguishable. The upper view is shown from the other side at close range, on this page. The little building is the Castle Gate depot; apparently no signals or other paraphernalia, excepting the station sign, have as yet been provided. The enlarged portion of the same photo below reveals the identical Porter engine (or a twin) pictured previously, still pushing the four antique flatcars. (Lower left, Wm. H. Jackson photo, Museum Coll.; others, John P. Soule photo, Univ. of Utah Coll.)

92-613 CASTLE GATE.

The area east of Castle Gate soon became a major coal producing region, served by both the Rio Grande Western and tributary Utah Railway. Mine facilities and terminal just east of Castle Gate, above, were photographed in the early 1890s. (State Historical Society of Colo.)

For amusement, the doctor told the *News*, the citizens of Green River

hang up an old pair of pants and see who can put the most holes through it while riding by at full gallop. The best pants-shooter in camp could put six holes through, with two guns, and he was the great man of the country.

Dr. Stroud decided that he did not want any more patients in Green River. No wonder it was this country that later spawned the "Wild Bunch".

Construction continued from both sides towards Green River. On March 8, 130 cars of material were forwarded through Grand Junction. On March 9 the line was completed to Crescent, 60.2 miles west of the border. The *News* for March 17 reported that "two trains loaded with material go to the front daily." The line was being laid at a rate of 1½ miles per day. By March 24 the line was only a couple of miles short of Green River, with the line from the west about fourteen miles on the other side. According to the *News* that day there was sufficient track material already at the "front" to complete the sixteen miles remaining.

On March 27, 1883, General Manager D. C. Dodge went through Grand Junction on his private train, headed west to participate in completion of the line. That same day the end of track was spiked down in Green River, 84.1 miles from the Colorado border.

On the afternoon of Friday, March 30, 1883, the last rail was laid 12.7 miles west of Green River and 0.3 Mile east of the siding known as Desert Switch, a total of 557.6 miles west of Denver. According to the *Deseret News* of Salt Lake City the event "occurred without the great display and outward rejoicing usual on such occasions." The editor added that, "It is a matter of no less importance on that account, however, being next in magnitude, so far as railroad affairs in this region are concerned, to the completion of the Central Pacific and Union Pacific lines, causing the spanning of the continent from sea to sea, by the iron-banded highways."

"FINISHED!" read the heading in the Grand Junction *News*. There followed an essay on the significance of completion of the Utah Extension, full of the florid phrases common to Victorian journalism.

At 6:30 a.m. on Thursday, April 5, the first passenger train wended its way westward over the still wobbly rails. It was a chartered special of two or three coaches carrying a colony of Mormons, en route from Chattanooga, Tennessee, who were headed for settlement in Utah under the supervision of Elder William Asper, others having departed at Salida for the San Luis Valley. That same day five cars of livestock were shipped out of Salt Lake City for Leadville, one of the first freights to cross the line in Utah. Regular passenger traffic on the new line began out of Denver on April 7, and out of Salt Lake on April 8, after some additional work on the track had been completed.

Perhaps one reason that the driving of the last spike connecting the lines building east and west received so little notice at the time was that it did not represent a completed line connecting with the Central Pacific. There was still no narrow gauge link between Salt Lake and Ogden, leaving shippers at the mercy of the Union Pacific's subsidiary, the Utah Central, at Salt Lake City. But the D&RG proceeded to remedy that immediately. On the evening of April 10, four hundred construction workmen who had just completed the line running east to Colorado arrived in Salt Lake City to begin work the following day on the line to Ogden. The issue of *Railroad Gazette* for May 4 reported the line completed ten miles northward to Wood's Cross, and on May 12, 1883, the narrow gauge road laid its rails into Ogden. There the Union Pacific attempted to keep the new line out of the joint UP-CP depot area, and managed to delay completion of the line until May 17, when the D&RG made arrangement with the Central Pacific in their mutual interest to allow a third rail to be laid down the CP tracks.

There was talk, of course, about a narrow gauge line clear to the Pacific Coast, and although it was never built, surveys were made.

Back in August, 1881, D&RGW Assistant Engineer F. C. Hand had examined Deep Creek Pass on the Nevada border west of Provo, and a survey party completed location on a strategic twenty miles of grade over this pass, filing the requisite right-of-way map with the Secretary of the Interior. Mr. Hand carried exploratory surveys far into Nevada, proposing to use Kingley and Egan Passes toward Eureka. Over $6,000 was subsequently spent on preliminary grading to hold Deep Creek Pass on a proposed line from Salt Lake to these Nevada mining camps.

At the same time, other narrow gauge lines were under construction, such as the Carson & Colorado, the Eureka & Palisade, and the Nevada Central, which offered the Rio Grande possible tributary routes. Meanwhile, clear out in California a company called the California & Nevada Railroad commenced tracklaying on San Francisco Bay in Oakland and built north and then easterly through the Berkeley Hills. A map that company published in 1882 showed a projected (but of course never built) through narrow gauge line crossing the Sierra Nevada Mountains east of Sonora, then running through Bodie and Candelaria and on to Utah to connect with the Rio Grande. Even after the D&RG had been standard gauged, a Rio Grande Western map of 1891 showed a line under construction beyond the Tintic Branch towards Deep Creek Pass and Nevada. Never completed, such lines were nevertheless on the engineers' drawing boards, and one wonders what William Jackson Palmer might have accomplished had he managed to retain control of the Denver & Rio Grande.

The completion of a track connection to the CP in Ogden did not mean that the narrow gauge main line was finished. Any new railway undergoes a process of appreciation before the counter-process of depreciation sets in — depreciation in this sense applies to the physical effect of the elements on the grade and track. The track is actually more vulnerable when brand new than after it has been in use for a few years. Fills need time to solid-

ify; new cuts have a tendency to slide down over the track, and the newly turned earth is unusually susceptible to erosion. In time, the earth will settle and the track will be adjusted, and eventually natural grasses will cover the raw earth and protect it from erosion. Engineers will learn by experience what timber trestles need to be replaced with more permanent iron structures, and where minor realignments of the track should be made. Just such a process was happening all along the line from Salida to Ogden.

Chief Engineer McMurtrie of the D&RG was especially anxious to eliminate the tortuous climb over the Cedar Creek Divide (Cerro Summit) west of Cimarron, and even before the line to Ogden was finished he was seeking an alternative. In January and February, 1883, when the Gunnison River was frozen and surveyors could walk over the ice to carry out their tasks, McMurtrie sent an engineering team down the lower Black Canon below the mouth of the Cimarron to ascertain whether a line from there to Delta could be built, thus eliminating the grades over the Cedar Creek Divide. For 11¼ miles the route provided no really serious difficulties, but below that, the grading would be so expensive as to be prohibitive. This line, of course, was never built, but it is indicative of the constant surveys undertaken to improve the route of the railway. For example, straightening of the line between Pueblo and Canon City had commenced in 1881 and continued in 1883.

On Marshall Pass, numerous improvements were necessary, especially the laying of heavier rail than the original 30 lb. steel, and the reduction of curvature from 24 to 15 degrees. This sort of work was commenced 3¼ miles west of Marshall Pass early in July, 1883, and involved the removal of a small landslide as well as the excavation of an impressive rock cut. East of the Pass, McMurtrie planned to put in stone arches (culverts) and replace trestles 14, 15, 16 and 18 with solid earth fills. Bridge 17 he proposed replacing with an iron trestle. In August, 1883, nine miles of 30 lb. steel over Marshall Pass was replaced with 45 lb. steel, with the lighter rail being relaid on the extension then being built from Maysville to Monarch. Such replacement of rail was carried on intermittently throughout the history of the railroad.

West of Montrose, major improvements were necessary along the lower Gunnison River. At about 5 a.m. on May 24, 1883, the east-bound passenger train approached the bridge over the Gunnison River at Robideau just west of Delta. The Gunnison was very high with the spring run-off, and Engineer W. Duncan slowed his engine to a walk as the train approached the bridge. Everything looked natural, and the locomotive crept out onto the wooden span. Suddenly, behind the engine the bridge began to collapse. Duncan threw on the airbrakes and grabbed the whistle cord. As the bridge went down it tilted the engine and tender backwards and threw them off on the upstream side, killing Duncan and Fireman Emory. The mail car and baggage car also went into the drink, the baggage car knocking a hole in the roof of the mail car in the process, a hole through which Route Agent J. E. Rudolph managed to swim to safety. The smoker hung on the brink, and no sooner had its passengers crawled out than it, too, fell in the river, lodging against a snag about three hundred feet downstream. The mail car, a complete wreck, was found a mile and a half downstream, and eventually was tied to some trees along the bank. Both the mail agent and the express agent were badly injured, and Brakeman Holbrook was thrown into the river, suffering a severe cut over one eye, but no passengers were casualties. The remainder of the bridge was somehow set afire in the wreck, and more than 100 feet of the span were destroyed. On the morning of June 1, 1883, the Robideau Bridge cost another life when Bridge Carpenter James Bowman, one of a crew trying to save what was left of the bridge from the high water, fell in the Gunnison, was swept away by the vicious current, and drowned. A better bridge was obviously needed, and by the end of 1883 McMurtrie had decided to install two 150-

East of Soldiers Summit the Price River Canon provided a scenic route of attractiveness to the tourist trade. In addition to the spectacular formations of Castle Gate, the remainder of the Price River valley was also rugged and colorful. On the page opposite, the narrow gauge tracks are shown at various points in the Canon; the formation in the center photo was publicized as the "Natural Castle". (Upper two, John P. Soule photos, Univ. of Utah Coll.; lower, C. R. Savage photo, Brigham Young Univ. Coll.) West of Soldiers Summit, and east of Provo, the line ran through a pretty valley called Spanish Fork Canon. In the view above, the well-known Salt Lake photographer C. W. Carter focused his camera along an unusually long stretch of tangent in the valley, with snow-flecked mountains in the distance. The rough pole ties of the newly-laid track have received only a minimum of dirt "ballast," but the alignment looks true. (LDS Church Information Office Coll.)

foot wooden Howe Truss spans at Robideau, although later still a steel bridge would be necessary.

A similar bridge over the Grand River just outside Grand Junction was to be replaced with three Howe Truss spans of 150 feet each. With the spring thaw, ice flowing down these streams could almost be guaranteed to take out a pile trestle, building up pressure upstream from the bridge as if behind a dam, until wood could withstand no more.

The most important change was in the lower Gunnison canyon at Bridgeport, roughly 25 miles southeast of Grand Junction. Here the original narrow gauge crossed the river four times to pass through a particularly narrow portion of the canon. To replace all of these pile bridges with more permanent Howe Truss spans was simply too expensive. It proved cheaper to stay on the northeast side of the Gunnison by employing a 2,950 foot curved tunnel, which aside from eliminating all four bridges shortened the line 2.1 miles, and eliminated 500 degrees of curvature. McMurtrie awarded contracts for the Bridgeport Tunnel on September 20, 1883. The contract called for completion on April 1, 1884, and after blasting their way through solid rock that did not require timbering, the contractors accomplished their task in the last week of March, 1884. Engine 280 was the first locomotive to pass through the tunnel, probably on Monday, March 25.

Slides as well as high water destroyed railroad bridges. On April 17, 1884, a rockfall smashed a bridge in the Black Canon east of Cimarron. The wrecking crew from Gunnison went down to repair the bridge, and the passenger train followed, the company intending to transfer the passengers across the break to another train on the other side. Several minor slides east of the Curecanti Needle had to be cleared first, and while the passenger train was waiting for the section gang to remove one of these from the track, yet another slide of rock and snow swept down the mountain, knocking the engine off the track and killing the engineer, Arthur Bratt.

"The fatality of engineers in the Black Canon during the past year has been enormous," commented the Gunnison *Review-Press*:

> It would seem that the faithful engineer upon whom so many lives depend and who is compelled to constantly risk his own life to save others, sooner or later meets with a violent death. Every few months the undertakers of Gunnison are called upon to lay out one of these boys and send his remains to sorrowing friends elsewhere.

Indeed, railroading in the Rocky Mountains was no child's play.

In repairing that Black Canon bridge, a minor change in alignment was made in the hope of diminishing the danger to trains from rockfalls and slides. Similarly in Utah such improvements were constantly being made. A new bridge was built over the Green River in 1885, and numerous track realignments were made. A snowshed proved necessary over Soldier Summit, and in 1887 a turntable covered with a snowshed was added to the facilities at the summit. The Grassy Trail area east of Price was a continuing source of concern. But on the whole, the Western's operation and maintenance problems proved less severe than those on the Colorado lines.

There were also continual improvements in the servicing facilities at major towns along the railroad. By 1884 the stone depot in Salida had been doubled in size, and the original 14-stall roundhouse had grown to 27 stalls. The railroad had also built two large stone shop buildings near the roundhouse. Other roundhouses on this line include a six-stall structure at Sargent at the western base of Marshall Pass, a ten-stall roundhouse at Gunnison, a five-stall engine house at Cimarron between the Black Canon and Cerro Summit, and an 11-stall engine house in Grand Junction, the latter handling both D&RG and D&RGW locomotives.

All of this work, of course, cost a fortune, and while Palmer and his men were engaged in improving the structure of the railway, the stock and bondholders, especially those in Europe and particularly the Scottish investors, were becoming increasingly restive and increasingly critical of the Palmer management.

It was 1878 all over again, but this time Palmer was not the winner. Without the support of the financial backers of the D&RG who wanted stringent economy, even to the extent of ruthless cutting of the salaries of operating officials, Palmer was wise enough to resign in August, 1883. But he remained president of the Utah lines. Subsequently the eastern and foreign interests who had won control of the Board of Trustees of the D&RG elected a Pennsylvanian, Frederick Lovejoy, to the presidency.

Lovejoy proceeded not only to cut expenditures right and left, but even welshed on provisions of the lease of the Western to the D&RG. Palmer was infuriated when the D&RG began firing officials friendly to Palmer and attempting to place its own officials in control of the Western in violation of the lease. Palmer's attorney advised the western to refuse to acknowledge the authority of officials such as Ricker who were illegally attempting to take control of the D&RGW in violation of Article 10. "The fight seems to be forced by the other side," Attorney Lyman Bass wrote D. C. Dodge on March 27. The latter had remained general manager of the Western even after Lovejoy had fired him from the D&RG. "They want the lease of the Western, and yet they don't want to abide by its terms," Bass told Dodge, and went on to say that the D&RG management had come to believe that it must "crush Genl. Palmer out in order to acquire the properties he represents." According to Bass,

> He is in their way. He obstructs their efforts to gobble everything. They have imbided prejudices easily, because they are anxious to imbide them. They tell all manner of lies to their adherents and retainers who circulate them as gospel truths. Now this "boom" of lying and misrepresentation, like other "booms" will have its day, and a short one, I think . . .

Bass advised Palmer and Dodge to yield nothing to the D&RG but to act carefully and keep the record straight so that every step could be defended.

> The other side have *rushed in* as if to bring an avalanche of

destruction in a day, but that is simple bombast . . . As to the Western road, I think you are master of the situation . . . Now Mr. Lovejoy may seek to interfere with your power . . . but Mr. Lovejoy is not a formidable adversary. He is hasty, forms his conclusions on half the facts, or no facts at all, and acts ill advisedly. He is as liable to take false steps as any man in so responsible a place I ever knew. He has a training that teaches him the arts of squeezing and bulldozing but with no high sense of absolute right and wrong.

Mr. Bass' assessment of Lovejoy was remarkably accurate, as events were to prove, although Bass underestimated Lovejoy's talent for mischief.

The dispute moved into the courts, where far from trying to break the lease, whose terms were very profitable for the Western, Palmer and his associates attempted to force D&RG compliance. Meanwhile, hearing talk that the D&RG was planning unilaterally to break the lease if it lost in court — which would also be illegal — and anticipating trouble on that account, in April Superintendent Bancroft of the Western moved all of his surplus locomotives at Grand Junction back to Green River, and thereafter interchanged with the D&RG at Grand Junction only as many cars as the D&RG sent out over the Western.

The situation was complicated by unusually heavy damage to track and bridges on both lines caused by heavy snows and the ensuing thaw and runoff. Marshall Pass and the Black Canon were intermittently closed, and the Robideau Bridge was still out. The Western suffered similarly on both sides of Soldier Summit. Bancroft reported on April 30 from Thistle Tank:

> We have had one continual succession of washouts since one week ago last Monday. Most every bridge through Price Canon & to Lower Crossing has been more or less damaged. Our track from Clear Creek to Pole Canon has been terribly washed. Bridges, loosing bents & piling & embankments either entirely carried

away or badly washed & had to be cribbed. The whole of the wall of the narrow place at the head of Red Narrows went out & the water run down through the cut five feet deep, washing our track very bad. We had to put in five cars of rails & build our wall on that. At one time it seemed to be impossible to repair this place & it being so narrow could not get around or over the wash. We have a wash here 300 feet long just east of the tank & very deep, no way to throw the track (to one side). We have been fighting the water all day to change the current in order to put in the fill. Think we have it secured now so we can commence on grade in a.m. . . . Our track is all out of shape all through the canon.

Bancroft had just heard that the D&RG was having its own trouble with slides in the Black Canon, and he added, "I think between God Almighty & Frederick Lovejoy they will bust up the D&RG."

As the court fight dragged on into May and June, Lovejoy tried to fire Palmer men from influential positions on both lines, and to run the Western merely as a division of the D&RG, again in violation of the lease. Western employees, however, remained loyal to Palmer's associates, and even in Colorado many D&RG men sympathized with Palmer. Finally, in the courts, the D&RG was fighting a losing case, and it was this which prompted Mr. Lovejoy to initiate the railroad war of 1884.

On Wednesday evening, July 2, 1884, the eastbound mail train rolled into Grand Junction off the Western, and before it could be switched for the return trip, Superintendent R. M. Ridgway ordered it seized, together with all the other Western engines and equipment in the town. At about the same time, D&RG employees cut the Western Union Telegraph wire between Grand Junction and points to the west. At 4 a.m. Thursday morning, Conductor Conlisk of the seized train managed to obtain a horse and, with a companion, started westward for the first telegraph station which still had a connection with Salt Lake in order to appraise

the Western management of the seizure. Four hours later, at 8 a.m. Thursday, a D&RG work train steamed westward out of Grand Junction, halting just short of the state line. There a D&RG section crew began tearing up track, working back towards the east. Accounts differ on how much track was torn up, but apparently at least a mile of rail was removed. Ridgway also ordered the removal of all locomotives and passenger cars from Grand Junction, including equipment seized from the Western, to points south of the river. Some of the equipment was reported standing just outside the yard limits below the bridge, and some was reported to have been removed as far south as Whitewater. Presumably the track removal and removal of equipment was to prevent a force of men from the Western from recovering it. As the final act in the drama, Ridgway placed armed guards at the border to prevent the Western from trying to relay the rail.

The Western's immediate reaction was to establish an operator in a tent at the end of track at the Utah border, and freight and passenger traffic in both directions had to move by wagon or stagecoach between Grand Junction and the border, which of course gave the freighting business a shot in the arm. The Western officials were all very angry at Ridgway, not at first believing that he had orders from Colorado Springs to take such steps. Bancroft had left Grand Junction just hours before the seizure, and wrote Dodge that Ridgeway's "only regret is that he did not capture me." The D&RGW management advised Western Union of the cutting of the telegraph wires, and that company agreed to handle D&RGW telegraph traffic over alternate routes, also planning steps against the D&RG. The Western Railway made no attempt to relay track or recapture its stolen equipment, relying instead on the courts. In fact, the effect of the track removal was to isolate Grand Junction entirely from rail traffic, as washouts prevented any rail movement on the main line east of Grand Junction, so that even prior to July 2 Grand Junction's only source of supply was shipment

eastward from Salt Lake City or other Utah points. Residents of Grand Junction dashed to their stores as soon as news of the track removal to the west became common knowledge, and by Saturday, July 5, there was already a shortage of flour.

Despite immediate and prospective hardships caused by the interruption of rail traffic both east and west, Grand Junction residents expected great benefits to flow from the conflict. "RAILROAD WAR" announced the headline on Saturday's paper, and the article that followed catalogued the benefits that might accrue to the town. First, the Western might be forced to build its own track from the border to Grand Junction; this would make the town a terminus of two competing lines rather than merely a stopping point on a through line, and there would be the prospect of a rate war on traffic between Grand Junction and Denver, on the one hand, and Grand Junction and Salt Lake, on the other, each city vying to capture Grand Junction's business with lower prices and the railroads competing with lower freight rates. Besides, the Western might chose to build on eastward to connect with the Denver, South Park & Pacific at Dillon, or perhaps over Ohio Pass to Baldwin. There were also rumors that the Burlington would build on to Grand Junction, and a railroad war between the D&RG and the D&RGW could only encourage such a move. Any such railroad construction would employ hundreds of men and teams, and help Grand Junction merchants out of their "present dull times." Furthermore, the railroad was attracting the attention of the whole state to Grand Junction, publicity which could not help being beneficial. Mayor Talbott and Sheriff Innes, consequently, remained neutral in the railroad war.

Not all Grand Junction residents were so complacent, however. Some were highly indignant at the action of Mr. Lovejoy and loudly voiced their protests. To placate them, Lovejoy was forced to propose handling freight and passenger traffic over the break by wagon, then by rail from end of track to Grand Junction, which would seem to have

Thistle (above) is the junction between the Sevier Valley line (the original projected route via Salina) and the main line over Soldiers Summit. This photo was apparently taken by Wm. H. Jackson in 1890, when the Sevier line was still narrow gauge — witness the dual gauge trackage and mixture of equipment. A clutch of narrow gauge engines can be detected in the roundhouse, at left. (State Historical Society of Colo.) In the rare view at right, an early D&RGW Ry. passenger train makes the station stop at Provo. Tenwheeler no. 158 heads a flat roofed baggage-mail, a baggage, three coaches and a sleeper. Plenty of passengers, depot-loungers, baggage carts and buggies are in evidence; the sign on the fence admonishes us to smoke "Seal of North Carolina" tobacco. The entire scene is dwarfed by the rugged mountains rising in the distance. (John P. Soule photo, Univ. of Utah Coll.)

eliminated the whole purpose of tearing up the track — that of hurting the Western. Still, the Western was supplying Grand Junction from the state line anyway, so the removal of rail seemed to have accomplished little, especially as the main line to Denver was in such bad condition that traffic there was interrupted. The Grand Junction *News* opposed any such transfer of traffic at the state line, fearing it would stimulate the beginning of supply stores and other necessary adjuncts at the break, "keeping the money and trade from the town which ought to come here."

Meanwhile, not only the Western in the person of D. C. Dodge, but even the Denver & Rio Grande's own bondholders applied on July 7 in the U. S. Circuit Court at Denver for a receivership. On Wednesday, July 9, one week after Dodge's initial request and the seizure of the Western mail train, W. S. Jackson, an old Palmer associate, was appointed receiver of the Denver & Rio Grande. Management of the railroad was out of the hands of Mr. Frederick Lovejoy at last, even though he remained president for some months.

The reprieve was timely. The Denver *News* reported Grand Junction to be on the verge of starvation, which, however, was an overstatement. While it was true that both flour and meat were unobtainable from the stores, most citizens in the town had hoarded stocks that would last from a week to a month, so the shortage was more apparent than real. The worst hardship, perhaps, was that the supply of soda water and beer had given out entirely, and these were not among the commodities that had been hoarded. Anyway, the newspaper reported on July 12 that wagon freighters were expected in that evening with flour, meats and a general line of supplies from the Utah line, and the fact that the regular mail train was running eastward every morning—with transfers necessary at several breaks in the line—indicated that the Marshall Pass-Black Canon line would soon be open to regular freight traffic.

Meanwhile the wagon freighters prospered. E. S. Rich of the Peo-

This is Salt Lake City in the early eighties. Above, East Temple Street was lined with an assortment of business houses, including a number of substantial brick buildings. A small horsecar is about to cross the street at the first intersection; in the background is the big ZCMI (Zion Co-operative Mercantile) building. In the left foreground a coalyard offers Red Canyon coal at $7.50 per ton delivered and a barber advertises 25¢ haircuts, while the Head Quarters Saloon is apparent across the street. (Cincinnati Historical Society, C. R. Savage photo). Below, a D&RGW Ry. passenger train waits at the depot, attended by a large flotilla of buggies and hacks. A sleeper and two coaches are at the back of the train; the consist may well be similar to that of the train shown at Provo. (John P. Soule photo, Univ. of Utah Coll.)

ple's Forwarding Company of Salt Lake had been en route to Whitewater to establish a wholesale house for the sale of hay and grain at the time the railroad war erupted, and he took advantage of the situation to establish a branch of his firm to handle freight and express from the state line to Grand Junction. On July 9 he sent seven freight teams west from Grand Junction on that mission. "Mr. Rich's forwarding company has proved a great blessing to our people here in bringing in supplies from the break," reported the *News*.

Others did not benefit from the situation. A Mr. Fred Rockwell had been shipping cattle from Utah to his range on Grand Mesa when the track was torn up, and he was caught just west of the break with all his stock. He consequently had to drive the cattle some thirty miles to Grand Junction, and then on to his range. But the situation to the East, caused by natural forces, was not much better. One passenger, a man named Carpenter, was obliged to travel not only by rail, but on foot, by stage and by rowboat to get over breaks in the D&RG line. (He negotiated the 45 miles from Delta to Grand Junction by rowboat down the turbulent Gunnison River.)

Receiver Jackson meanwhile had crews working to get the main line from Denver in operating condition, and on Monday, July 14, D&RG crews began relaying the track torn up at the state line. At 5:30 p.m. that day the first train from the west, a freight, steamed into Grand Junction, the engine decorated with green bows and the word "Victory" attached in large letters to the headlight. Its whistle screamed and everyone shook hands with enthusiasm. The Western's Superintendent Bancroft, Assistant Superintendent Horner, Mr. Eccles, Chief Engineer McMurtrie and other Western officials arrived by a special train from Salt Lake Wednesday and were greeted by the Grand Junction cornet band and the town's prominent citizens.

Rail traffic from the west was very lively after the rail was relaid. Over two hundred empty freight cars were on the Western when the track was torn up and these were now rushed into Grand Junction along with many loads.

One side effect of the break was reported on July 19. While traffic was stalled on the Western, some of that road's officials discovered that a number of freight cars side-tracked at Green River were being systematically looted, as one might expect in that tough town. The railroad engaged a Captain Hawley of the Rocky Mountain Detective Agency of Denver to run down the thieves, and shortly thereafter the detective hauled one J. M. Crowley before Justice Frazier in Grand Junction. Hawley had found a barrel of stolen whiskey and seven thousand stolen cigars in Crowley's possession.

By the latter part of July temporary repairs had been made to the Robideau Bridge west of Delta and traffic could roll through from Denver to Ogden. A week later the long-overdue pay car arrived and paid the D&RG men in Grand Junction for the month of May. Among his other practices Mr. Lovejoy had failed to pay his own men. As D. C. Dodge had commented to Palmer back in June, "Lovejoy has not only ruined the business of the D&RG but has ruined its credit also, and no one has any confidence in his promises." Both Palmer's group and the D&RG's own employees had a much better opinion of Receiver Jackson.

In September, the D&RG announced that it would spend $100,000 in rebuilding the bridge in the Black Canon that had been crushed by the rockfall in the spring, as well as the bridge at Robideau, both of which had been replaced with temporary structures. These temporary spans, once the spring floods had diminished, sufficed to carry current traffic, which included two emigrant trains carrying settlers from Idaho and Utah southeast to the San Luis Valley and New Mexico. Now that Jackson was in control of the Colorado lines, relations between the two companies were restored to a more reasonable plane.

The results of the "railroad war," which might be more accurately described as Mr. Lovejoy's temporary insanity, probably were permanently damaging to both railroads. Prior to July 2, the D&RG-D&RGW had a profitable traffic arrangement with the Burlington at Denver for through freight to the west. The interruptions caused by snows, slides and washouts had already seriously interrupted that traffic, and the removal of track on July 3 was the last straw. The Burlington proceeded to negotiate an alternate agreement with the Santa Fe for through traffic to the Pacific coast, and the Rio Grande lines were unable to recapture this traffic after rail was replaced. Consequently far from improving Grand Junction's situation, the "railroad war" of 1884 had in fact permanently damaged it. Mr. Lovejoy's career with the Rio Grande was at an end and he soon resigned, for not even the bondholders who had opposed Palmer's management could tolerate such damage as their own nominee had caused. If the stock and bond holders had continued to support Palmer, they might have fared better after all.

After the major interruptions of 1884, through trains between Denver and Ogden operated with only the minor interruptions that were a part of the operating problems of any railroad. The through passenger train over the route was known as the *Atlantic Express* when eastbound and the *Pacific Express* when westbound. Schedules varied down through the years. As of the August 19, 1884 timecard the train left Denver at 7:40 a.m., arriving at Salida at 4:40 p.m., Gunnison at 9:10, and Montrose at 12:25. The train stopped at Grand Junction at 3:20 a.m. and Green River at 7:30 a.m. the second day. If on time the train was passing through scenic Castle Gate at 10:50 a.m. and went over Soldier Summit around noon, reaching Provo at 2:35, Salt Lake City at 4:40, and Ogden at 6 p.m. The total trip thus took a minimum of 34 hours and twenty minutes to cover 771.3 miles.

Eastbound passengers from Central Pacific Train No. 1 arrived at Ogden at 7:55 a.m. and departed eastward on the Denver & Rio Grande Western at 9:10 a.m., arriving at Salt Lake City at 10:30, Provo at 12:25, Castle Gate at 4 p.m., and Green River at 7:20 p.m.

The D&RGW Ry. built an ornate bathing pavilion and beach facilities at Lake Park, a point midway between Salt Lake City and Ogden, where the tracks passed close to Great Salt Lake. It proved an attraction — and provided trainloads of patrons — for a number of years. In these 1890 views, newly painted and lettered Rio Grande Western tenwheeler no. 20 (ex-no. 158) poses above, while eightwheeler no. 15 (ex-no. 108) appears below. Narrow gauge operation would end shortly thereafter. (Upper, C. W. Carter photo, LDS Church Information Office Coll.; lower, Utah State Historical Society.)

In Grand Junction the train was handed over from the Western to the D&RG at one minute before midnight. On the second day the Atlantic Express arrived at Montrose at 3:46 a.m., Cimarron at 5:10, Gunnison at 7:11, Salida at five minutes after noon, and Denver at 9 p.m. that night. On the eastern end, the Rio Grande connected with the Santa Fe, Chicago, Kansas & Nebraska (Rock Island) and Missouri Pacific at Pueblo and with the Union Pacific, Burlington & Missouri River and Kansas Pacific Railroads at Denver. At Ogden, the Rio Grande trains connected with the Central Pacific for through traffic to the Pacific Coast, or travelers could take the Utah & Northern or the Oregon Short Line for points in Oregon, Idaho or Montana.

Of course due to the difference in gauge, no through cars were run over the Rio Grande; travelers had to change trains at each end of the line during the 1880s. Oddly enough, the one exception to this rule was in freight equipment, for certain refrigerator cars were indeed interchanged from standard to narrow gauge or vice versa on a through basis. These specially designed cars were simply lifted from standard to narrow gauge trucks, or the reverse, at Denver or Ogden, and were commonly seen on the narrow gauge main line in freight trains during those years.

The regular equipment on the narrow gauge passenger trains included a mail car, a baggage car, coaches, cars with Horton patent reclining chairs, and Pullman buffet sleeping cars. The latter, introduced in 1883, were described by the Denver *Republican* as a

> combination of dining and sleeping cars, and at the buffet the hungry passenger can always secure an appetizing lunch, a fragrant cigar and a cup of coffee, tea, chocolate or a glass of Apolinaris, Hathorn, or lemonade. Comfort, convenience and artistic beauty characterize the internal arrangement and finish of these coaches. An electric bell connects each section in the car with the buffet. The rates for refreshments are nominal, and the price for accommodations is no more than in other

> Pullmans . . . Silver table-ware, snowy linen and polite service add to the pleasure of the traveler who journeys in a buffet car over the popular Denver and Rio Grande Railway.

For the less affluent trade, the D&RG Burnham Shops later that year turned out a number of "Emigrant Sleepers" which the *Republican* also described:

> The exterior finish of the cars is equal in every respect to a Palace Pullman. Allen paper wheels are placed under the cars, which rest on Pullman trucks, thus securing the maximum of ease and comfort. The interior is a model of neatness and convenience. There is a cooking range at each end of the car for the accommodation of those who desire to prepare their own meals, there are receptacles for ice water, patent ventilators, a spacious closet lavatory, and, in fact, everything that the ingenuity of the car-builder could devise to add to the comfort of the passenger. These sleepers are longer than the regular passenger coaches and have sleeping accommodations for 28 passengers each. The berths are capacious and ingeniously constructed, and can be made as comfortable as those in any sleeper. The interior decoration corresponds in elegance with the handsome exterior. The windows are large and filled with single planes of glass, free from flaws and giving an unobstructed view. Sliding shutters are added, a convenience wanting in the majority of emigrant sleepers. Lighted by large and elegant lamps, heated, when heat is necessary, by improved furnaces, ventilated in the most approved fashion, clean and cool, these cars give the maximum of comfort at the minimum of cost to those who patronize them.

The first of these cars were apparently put in service on September 20, 1883. All of this equipment, of course, was painted a Tuscan (maroon) red, highly varnished, with elaborate gold-leaf lettering and striping. When new, they were unbelievably elegant. As time went on the cars would become streaked with soot, and subsequent economy-minded officials of the D&RG tend-

ed to decrease the amount of gold-leaf decoration.

Through the Royal Gorge, over Marshall Pass and through the Black Canon, four open-top excursion cars were available for use on the through trains in appropriate weather. These were generally coupled to the rear of the train, and gave the passengers a magnificent view of the scenery, at the cost of sunburn, windburn, cinders in the eyes, soot on the clothing, and perhaps a few drops of rain. One could always, of course, return to a Pullman or a coach.

A subsidiary of the railroad, the Rio Grande Hotel Company, operated hotels and eating houses on the line, and at some locations there were independent "dining rooms" of which the management approved and listed in railroad literature. Those on the main line operated by the Rio Grande Hotel Company included the Depot Hotel and Eating House in Pueblo, the Monte Christo (sic) Hotel and Eating House built in 1883 in Salida, the Black Canon Hotel and Eating House at Cimarron, and the Eating House in Grand Junction. In Gunnison, private interests opened the magnificent, four-story LaVeta Hotel in 1884, and the railroad subsequently built a spur line which ran past the south side of the hotel. The railroad also established its Gunnison passenger station in the hotel adjacent to the railroad track, so that at Gunnison passengers could eat in the Hotel's dining room if they so wished.

Shadrach K. Hooper, who replaced F. C. Nims as General Passenger and Ticket Agent of the D&RG during the railroad war of 1884, changed Nims' "Scenic Line of America" slogan to read "Scenic Line of the World," and adopted the Curecanti Needle in the Black Canon as the central symbol of the new herald. (This design would last until the mid-1920's.)

From time to time passenger and freight traffic was interrupted by inclement weather. Washouts, slides, deep snow on Marshall Pass provided continuing operating problems for the Rio Grande The railroad not infrequently spent $100,-000 or more to keep the Marshall Pass line open through a single win-

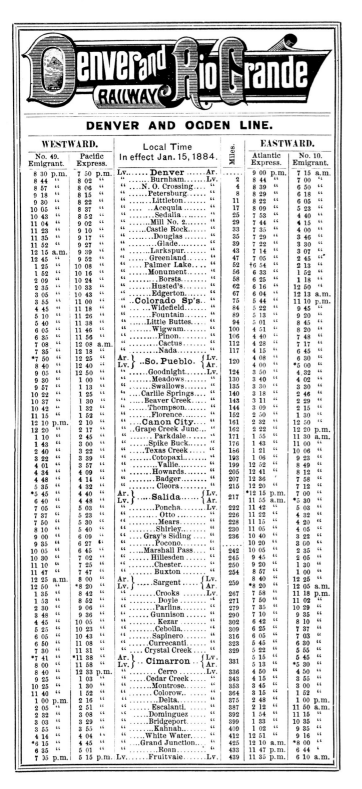

Denver and Rio Grande RAILWAY

DENVER AND OGDEN LINE.

WESTWARD.		Local Time		EASTWARD.	
No. 49. Emigrant.	Pacific Express.	In effect Jan. 15, 1884.	Miles.	Atlantic Express.	No. 10. Emigrant.
8 30 p.m.	7 50 p.m.	Lv....Denver......Ar.	.....	9 00 p.m.	7 15 a.m.
8 44 "	8 02 "	"....Burnham......Lv.	2	8 44 "	7 00 "
8 57 "	8 06 "	"..N. O. Crossing....	4	8 39 "	6 50 "
9 18 "	8 15 "	"...Petersburg.....	8	8 29 "	6 18 "
9 30 "	8 22 "	"....Littleton.....	11	8 22 "	6 05 "
10 05 "	8 37 "	"....Acequia.....	17	8 09 "	5 23 "
10 43 "	8 52 "	"....Sedalia.....	25	7 53 "	4 40 "
11 04 "	9 02 "	"....Mill No. 2....	29	7 44 "	4 15 "
11 23 "	9 10 "	"...Castle Rock....	33	7 35 "	4 00 "
11 35 "	9 17 "	"....Douglas.....	35	7 29 "	3 46 "
11 52 "	9 27 "	"....Glade.....	39	7 22 "	3 30 "
12 15 a.m.	9 39 "	"....Larkspur.....	43	7 14 "	3 07 "
12 45 "	9 52 "	"....Greenland.....	47	7 05 "	2 45 "
1 25 "	10 08 "	"...Palmer Lake....	52	†6 54 "	2 13 "
1 52 "	10 16 "	"....Monument.....	56	6 33 "	1 52 "
2 09 "	10 24 "	"....Borsts.....	58	6 25 "	1 18 "
2 35 "	10 33 "	"....Husted's.....	62	6 16 "	12 50 "
3 05 "	10 43 "	"....Edgerton.....	67	6 04 "	12 13 a.m.
3 55 "	11 00 "	"..Colorado Sp's..	75	5 44 "	11 10 p.m.
4 45 "	11 18 "	"....Widefield.....	84	5 22 "	9 45 "
5 10 "	11 26 "	"....Fountain.....	89	5 13 "	9 20 "
5 40 "	11 38 "	"..Little Buttes....	94	5 01 "	8 45 "
6 05 "	11 46 "	"....Wigwam.....	100	4 51 "	8 20 "
6 35 "	11 56 "	"....Pinon.....	106	4 40 "	7 48 "
7 08 "	12 08 a.m.	"....Cactus.....	112	4 28 "	7 17 "
7 35 "	12 18 "	"....Nada.....	117	4 15 "	6 45 "
*7 50 "	12 25 "	Ar.}..So. Pueblo..{Lv.	120	4 08 "	6 30 "
8 40 "	12 40 "	Lv.} {Ar.		4 00 "	*5 00 "
9 05 "	12 50 "	"....Goodnight....Lv.	124	3 50 "	4 32 "
9 30 "	1 00 "	"....Meadows.....	130	3 40 "	4 02 "
9 57 "	1 13 "	"....Swallows.....	135	3 30 "	3 30 "
10 22 "	1 25 "	"...Carlile Crossing..	140	3 18 "	2 46 "
10 37 "	1 30 "	"..Beaver Creek...	143	3 11 "	2 29 "
10 42 "	1 32 "	"....Thompson.....	144	3 09 "	2 15 "
11 15 "	1 52 "	"....Florence.....	152	2 50 "	1 30 "
12 10 p.m.	2 10 "	"...Canon City...	161	2 32 "	12 50 "
12 20 "	2 17 "	"..Grape Creek Junc..	162	2 22 "	12 20 p.m.
1 10 "	2 45 "	"....Parkdale.....	171	1 55 "	11 30 a.m.
1 43 "	3 00 "	"...Spike Buck....	176	1 43 "	11 00 "
2 40 "	3 22 "	"..Texas Creek....	186	1 21 "	10 06 "
3 22 "	3 39 "	"....Cotopaxi.....	193	1 06 "	9 23 "
4 01 "	3 57 "	"....Vallie.....	199	12 52 "	8 49 "
4 34 "	4 09 "	"....Howards.....	205	12 41 "	8 12 "
4 48 "	4 14 "	"....Badger.....	207	12 36 "	7 58 "
5 35 "	4 32 "	"....Cleora.....	215	12 20 "	7 12 "
*5 45 "	4 40 "	Ar.}..Salida..{Lv.	217	*12 15 p.m.	7 00 "
6 40 "	4 48 "	Lv.} {Ar.		11 55 a.m.	*5 30 "
7 05 "	5 03 "	"....Poncha....Lv.	222	11 42 "	5 03 "
7 37 "	5 23 "	"....Otto.....	226	11 22 "	4 32 "
7 50 "	5 30 "	"....Mears.....	228	11 15 "	4 20 "
8 10 "	5 40 "	"....Shirley.....	230	11 05 "	4 05 "
9 00 "	6 09 "	"..Gray's Siding....	236	10 40 "	3 22 "
9 35 "	6 27 "	"....Pocono.....	.....	10 20 "	3 00 "
10 05 "	6 45 "	"...Marshall Pass...	242	10 05 "	2 35 "
10 30 "	7 02 "	"....Hillesden.....	245	9 45 "	2 05 "
11 10 "	7 25 "	"....Chester.....	250	9 20 "	1 30 "
11 47 "	7 47 "	"....Buxton.....	254	8 57 "	1 00 "
12 25 a.m.	8 00 "	Ar.}..Sargent..{Lv.	259	8 40 "	12 25 "
12 50 "	*8 20 "	Lv.} {Ar.		*8 20 "	12 05 a.m.
1 35 "	8 42 "	"....Crooks.....Lv.	267	7 58 "	11 18 p.m.
1 53 "	8 52 "	"....Doyle.....	271	7 50 "	11 02 "
2 30 "	9 06 "	"....Parlins.....	279	7 35 "	10 29 "
3 48 "	9 36 "	"....Gunnison.....	290	7 10 "	9 35 "
4 45 "	10 05 "	"....Kezar.....	302	6 42 "	8 10 "
5 25 "	10 23 "	"....Cebolla.....	309	6 25 "	7 37 "
6 05 "	10 43 "	"....Sapinero.....	316	6 05 "	7 03 "
6 50 "	11 08 "	"....Currecanti.....	323	5 45 "	6 30 "
7 30 "	11 31 "	"..Crystal Creek....	329	5 22 "	5 55 "
*7 41 "	*11 38 "	Ar.} Cimarron {Lv.	331	5 15 "	5 45 "
8 00 "	11 58 "	Lv.} {Ar.		5 13 "	*5 30 "
8 40 "	12 33 p.m.	"....Cerro.....Lv.	336	4 50 "	4 50 "
9 25 "	1 03 "	"...Cedar Creek....	343	4 15 "	3 55 "
10 25 "	1 30 "	"....Montrose.....	353	3 45 "	3 00 "
11 40 "	1 52 "	"....Colorow.....	364	3 15 "	1 52 "
1 00 p.m.	2 16 "	"....Delta.....	375	2 48 "	1 00 p.m.
2 05 "	2 51 "	"....Escalanti.....	387	2 12 "	11 50 a.m.
2 32 "	3 08 "	"....Dominguez.....	392	1 54 "	11 15 "
3 03 "	3 29 "	"....Bridgeport.....	399	1 33 "	10 35 "
3 55 "	3 55 "	"....Kahnah.....	409	1 02 "	9 35 "
4 14 "	4 04 "	"...White Water....	412	12 51 "	9 16 "
*6 15 "	4 45 "	"..Grand Junction..	423	12 10 a.m.	*8 00 "
6 35 "	5 01 "	"....Roan.....	433	11 47 p.m.	6 44 "
7 35 p.m.	5 15 p.m.	Lv....Fruitvale....Lv.	439	11 35 p.m.	6 10 a.m.

DENVER AND OGDEN LINE.—Continued.

WESTWARD.		STATIONS.		EASTWARD.	
No 49. Emigrant.	Pacific Express.		Miles.	Atlantic Express.	No. 10. Emigrant.
7 40 p.m.	5 31 p.m.	Lv....Crevasse....Lv.	446	11 20 p.m.	5 35 a.m.
8 08 "	5 44 "	"....Shale.....	452	11 05 "	5 05 "
8 40 "	5 55 "	"....Excelsior.....	457	10 54 "	4 40 "
9 15 "	6 08 "	"....Acheron.....	463	10 38 "	4 02 "
10 12 "	6 32 "	"...West Water....	474	10 12 "	3 00 "
10 45 "	6 45 "	"....Cottonwood....	479	9 57 "	2 28 "
11 55 "	7 08 "	"....Cisco.....	490	9 32 "	1 25 a.m.
1 23 a.m.	7 45 "	"....Sagers.....	507	8 50 "	11 55 p.m.
2 10 "	8 02 "	"...Thompson's....	515	8 30 "	11 00 "
2 39 "	8 15 "	"....Crescent.....	521	8 15 "	10 22 "
3 17 "	8 30 "	"...Little Grand...	529	7 57 "	9 33 "
3 55 "	8 45 "	"....Solitude.....	537	7 40 "	8 45 "
5 15 "	9 15 "	"...Green River....	545	7 20 "	7 20 "
6 30 "	9 45 "	"....Desert.....	558	6 50 "	5 30 "
7 45 "	9 55 "	Ar.}Lower Price Cros'.{Lv.	570	*6 25 "	3 45 "
*8 00 "	*10 15 "	Lv.} {Ar.		6 10 "	.....
9 00 "	10 43 "	"...Grassy Trail...Lv.	582	5 44 "	2 37 "
9 45 "	11 07 "	"...Sunny Side....	591	5 22 "	1 44 "
10 35 "	11 30 "	"....Farnham.....	600	5 00 "	12 48 p.m.
1 05 p.m.	12 10 a.m.	"...Castle Gate....	624	4 00 "	10 25 a.m.
*3 55 "	1 35 "	"Pleasant Valley Junc."	637	3 20 "	9 10 "
4 30 "	1 55 "	"..Soldier Summit...	644	2 55 "	7 45 "
5 20 "	2 35 "	"...Clear Creek....	651	2 15 "	6 45 "
6 10 "	2 57 "	"....Mill Fork....	658	1 55 "	6 00 "
7 10 "	3 30 "	"....Thistle.....	669	1 25 "	5 00 "
8 05 "	4 00 "	"...Spanish Fork...	680	12 55 "	4 00 "
8 35 "	4 10 "	"....Springville.....	684	12 45 "	3 20 "
.....	4 21 "	Ar.}....Provo....{Lv.	689	12 30 "	2 30 "
9 15 "	4 23 "	Lv.} {Ar.		*12 10 p.m.	.....
10 00 "	4 46 "	"..Battle Creek..Lv.	699	11 51 a.m.	1 35 "
10 17 "	4 55 "	"..American Fork..	702	11 43 "	1 09 "
10 35 "	5 03 "	"....Lehi.....	705	11 35 "	12 45 a.m.
11 45 "	5 40 "	"....Draper.....	718	11 05 "	11 45 p.m.
12 20 a.m.	5 56 "	"..Bingham Junction..	724	10 50 "	11 09 "
1 15 "	6 20 "	Ar.}..Salt Lake..{Lv.	735	10 30 "	10 00 "
1 50 "	6 30 "	Lv.} {Ar.		10 20 "	9 30 "
2 35 "	6 51 "	"...Wood Cross..Lv.	743	10 03 "	8 41 "
3 12 "	7 07 "	"...Farmington....	750	9 50 "	8 05 "
3 32 "	7 15 "	"....Kaysville.....	754	9 43 "	7 45 "
4 26 "	7 40 "	"....Hooper.....	764	9 23 "	6 47 "
5 00 a.m.	7 55 a.m.	Ar....Ogden....Lv.	771	9 10 a.m.	6 10 p.m.

Passengers holding Second-Class tickets are carried in handsome Coaches attached to Express Trains. At present Third-Class through Passengers are also transported on Express Trains in Free Emigrant Sleepers.

Ogden, Bingham and Springville Local Trains.

NORTHWARD.		STATIONS.		SOUTHWARD.	
Bingham Passenger.	Springville Passenger.		Miles.	Springville Passenger.	Bingham Passenger.
	7 25 a.m.	Lv....Springville...Ar.	87	7 20 p.m.	
	7 39 "	"....Provo....Lv.	73	7 06 "	
	8 02 "	"...Battle Creek...	73	6 43 "	
	8 10 "	"..American Fork...	69	6 33 "	
	8 20 "	"....Lehi.....	66	6 25 "	
	8 51 "	"....Draper.....	53	5 52 "	
2 30 p.m.		"....Bingham....Ar.	63		9 10 a.m.
3 30 "	9 07 "	"..Bingham Junction..Lv.	47	5 35 "	7 55 "
4 00 "	9 35 "	Ar.}..Salt Lake..{Lv.	36	5 10 "	7 25 "
4 10 "	9 40 "	Lv.} {Ar.		5 00 "	8 00 p.m.
4 35 "	10 03 "	"...Woods Cross..Lv.	28	4 35 "	7 40 "
4 51 "	10 31 "	"...Farmington....	22	4 18 "	7 22 "
5 00 "	10 31 "	"....Kaysville.....	17	4 10 "	7 13 "
5 25 "	10 59 "	"....Hooper.....	7	3 45 "	6 47 "
5 40 p.m.	11 15 a.m.	Ar....Ogden....Lv.		3 30 p.m.	6 30 p.m.

SAN LUIS BRANCH.

SOUTHWARD.	STATIONS.		NORTHWARD.
Passenger.		Miles.	Passenger.
..... 7 15 p.m.	Lv....Denver....Ar.		7 10 a.m. .....
12 55 a.m.	"..South Pueblo.."	120	1 55 "
7 30 "	"....Salida..."	217	5 35 "
8 55 "	"....Mears...."	228	4 20 "
9 22 "	"..Poncha Pass..Lv.	231	3 50 "
9 47 "	"...Round Hill...	234	3 25 "
11 10 "	"...Villa Grove...	247	2 20 "
12 10 p.m.	Ar..Hot Springs..Lv.	255	12 50 p.m.

The timetable above shows the through schedules as of January 15, 1884. Curiously, the Royal Gorge is not even mentioned. To see the scenery along the entire route, a tourist would have to ride both directions; either way, it was a 36 hour trip on the "Pacific" or "Atlantic" Express. But consider nos. 49 and 10, the "Emigrant", which consumed 4 nights and three days going from Denver to Ogden — 80 hours for 771 miles! This must have been a very leisurely "mixed" train! (Museum Coll.) The train order opposite reflects the dispute between the opposing management factions attempting to operate the D&RGW Ry. at the time. The existence of rival timetables must've livened up the road's operation no little bit! (State Historical Society of Colo.)

ter. The 23 snowsleds over the pass were a partial solution, but they were susceptable to fire, and by the summer of 1889 at least five sheds had burned that would not be rebuilt. Snow removal in the 1880s was generally accomplished by wedge plows of varying sizes mounted over the pilots of engines, and by flanger-spreader cars towed by an engine which cleared the snow from between the rails as well as pushing it out with wing plows from the side of the track. It was not until 1889 that the D&RG purchased its own rotary plows. The Leslie Brothers Manufacturing Company of Paterson, New Jersey, shipped Rotary OM in January, and Rotary ON in February. The possession of these rotaries diminished the need for snowsheds, but the long shed at the summit of Marshall Pass remained as long as the railroad. However, rotaries, although effective in clearing drifted snow, were of limited use in clearing slides, for slides frequently contained rocks or trees that would damage the rotary blades, and consequently had to be cleared by being shoveled out by

hand or with the use of wedge plows on engines.

Snow was a frequent source of derailments, together with moisture-softened track. Lewis Lathrop recalled one flanger run from Gunnison through the Black Canon and over Cerro Summit to the Cedar Creek Wye and return. The crew made the run in good time, clearing snow from the line over the Squaw Hills, but as they ran down the west side of Cerro Summit the fireman suddenly let out a yell and jumped from the engine, and before Lathrop could react a slide slammed into the train, knocking the flanger and caboose fifty feet down the mountain side. The tender had been sheared off from the engine coupling, and rolled over, but the locomotive, brought to a stop by the impact of the snow, was still on the rails and started to move forward. Lathrop, picking himself up out of a snowdrift and brushing the snow from his eyes, jumped up and ran after the engine, which was picking up speed on the down grade. He barely managed to grab the hand-holds and pull himself into the fire-

man's side of the cab. But this was a deckless cab, and to get to the throttle and brake, he had to squeeze over the top of the boiler. Before the runaway was going fast enough to derail, Lathrop had managed to reverse it and brake it to a stop. Then he ran the tenderless-engine back upgrade to pick up his fireman and train crew, whose jaws gaped with astonishment when they saw this strange apparition approaching. They then all climbed onto the engine and Lathrop ran down to the station at the Cedar Creek wye. The operator there was so astonished at the sight of an engine running along without a tender that he actually rubbed his eyes. While the conductor wired in a report of the wreck, Lathrop parked the engine on a siding, blocked the wheels, dumped the fire, blew the water out of the boiler, and drained the pipes so they wouldn't freeze. The engine had not been damaged, and the tender could be easily repaired.

Another wreck on Cerro Summit occurred in 1887 when an engine tried to buck its way through what appeared to be a snowdrift, but instead was solid ice camouflaged with a frosting of fresh snow. The engine struck this and turned over. (Many years later the smashed box oil headlight from this wreck was recovered from Cerro Summit, and it is now on display at the Colorado Railroad Museum.)

But wrecks were not the only hazard facing crews on the Rio Grande lines in narrow gauge days. As indicated earlier, the tough Green River country of Utah was a source of outlaw activity and it was here that the loose collection of hoodlums known collectively as the "Wild Bunch" got their start. Their first train robbery was on the D&RG narrow gauge.

At 3:45 a.m. November 3, 1887, the eastbound *Atlantic Express*, running late on a brightly moonlit night, negotiated the lower canon of the Gunnison River five miles south of Grand Junction. Suddenly Engineer Malloy saw a pile of rocks and ties on the track surmounted by a red brakeman's lantern—which could mean a washout, a slide, or

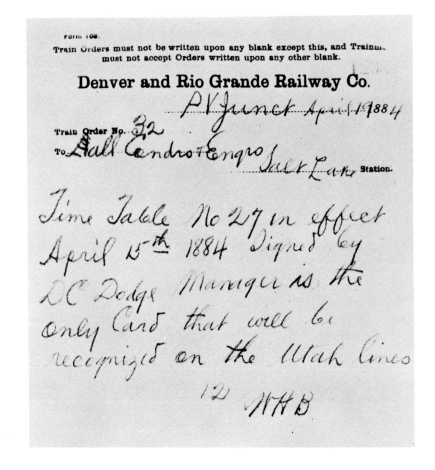

PACIFIC JUNCTION and OMAHA
TO
SAN FRANCISCO
—VIA—
Burlington & Missouri River, Denver & Rio Grande and Central Pacific Railroads.
No Change of Cars of any class between DENVER and OGDEN.

Mls	STATIONS.	Route.	Pacific Exp., Daily.	Emigrant. Daily.
0	Lv. Pacific Junction..	..B. & M. R.R..	8 25 a.m.	8 25 a.m.
9	Ar. Oreapolis	"	9 00 "	9 00 "
0	Lv. Omaha............	..B. & M. R.R..	10 05 a.m.	10 05 a.m.
53	Ar. Lincoln	"	11 45 "	11 45 "
0	Lv. Omaha...	..B. & M. R.R..	....	....
16	Ar. Oreapolis	"	....	....
9	Lv. Oreapolis	..B. & M. R.R..	9 00 a.m.	9 00 a.m.
60	Ar. Lincoln	"	11 20* "	11 20* "
60	Lv. Lincoln	"	12 05 p.m.	12 05 p.m.
157	Ar. Hastings.........	"	3 45 "	3 45 "
157	Lv. Hastings.........	"	4 00 "	4 00 "
289	Ar. McCook	"	9 45 "	9 45 "
289	Lv. McCook	"	8 55 "	8 55 "
543	Ar. Denver..........	"	7 00 a.m.	7 00 a.m.
0	Lv. Denver..........	D. & R. G. R.R.	8 20 "	8 20 "
52	" Palmer Lake.....	"	10 32†	10 32†
75	Ar. Colorado Springs.	"	11 19 "	11 19 "
75	Lv. Colorado Springs.	"	11 22 "	11 23 "
120	Ar. South Pueblo....	"	12 50* p.m.	12 50* p.m.
120	Lv. South Pueblo....	"	1 10 "	1 10 "
161	" Canon City......	"	2 40 "	2 40 "
217	Ar. Salida..........	"	†3 00 "	†3 00 "
217	Lv. Salida..........	"	5 10 "	5 10 "
242	" Marshall Pass....	"	6 55 "	6 55 "
259	Ar. Sargent	"	*8 00 "	*8 00 "
259	Lv. Sargent	"	8 20 "	8 20 "
290	" Gunnison........	"	9 30 "	9 30 "
331	Ar. Cimarron	"	11 23 "	11 23 "
331	Lv. Cimarron	"	11 28 "	11 28 "
353	" Montrose........	"	12 50 a.m.	12 50 a.m.
375	" Delta..........	"	1 38 "	1 38 "
425	Ar. Grand Junction..	"	3 45 "	3 45 "
425	Lv. Grand Junction..	D. R. G. W. R'y	3 55 "	3 55 "
545	Ar. Green River.....	"	*8 10 "	*8 10 "
545	Lv. Green River.....	"	8 35 "	8 35 "
637	Ar. P. V. Junction...	"	12 30 p.m.	12 30 p.m.
637	Lv. P. V. Junction...	"	12 30 "	12 30 "
684	" Springville	"	2 30 "	2 30 "
689	Ar. Provo...........	"	*2 40 "	*2 40 "
689	Lv. Provo...........	"	3 00 "	3 00 "
724	" Bingham Junc....	"	4 12 "	4 12 "
735	Ar. Salt Lake..	"	4 35 "	4 35 "
735	Lv. Salt Lake	"	4 40 "	4 40 "
771	Ar. Ogden...........	"	*6 00 "	*6 00 "
0	Lv. Ogden...........	Cent. Pac. R.R.	6 00 "	6 00 "
25	" Corinne..........	"	7 05 "	7 05 "
92	" Kelton...........	"	10 25 "	10 25 "
276	" Elko.............	"	*7 55 a.m.	*7 55 a.m.
308	" Palisade.........	"	9 25 "	9 25 "
359	" Battle Mount.....	"	11 17 "	11 17 "
419	" Winnemucca	"	1 35 p.m	1 35 p.m.
589	" Reno.............	"	*8 40 "	*8 40 "
624	" Truckee..........	"	11 10 "	11 10 "
689	" Colfax...........	"	4 00 a.m.	4 00 a.m
743	" Sacramento	"	*7 20 "	*7 20 "
828	" Oakland Pier.....	"	10 45 "	10 45 "
833	Ar. San Francisco....	"	11 10 "	11 10 "
....	Ar. Los Angeles.....	"	7 20 "	7 20 "

LAKE PARK.

THE GREAT SALT LAKE
BATHING STATION

Of the DENVER & RIO GRANDE RAILROAD, midway between Salt Lake City and Ogden, is now open for the accommodation of visitors. Unequaled Restaurant and Exchange, Bath Rooms completely furnished, stationary wash-stands, shower-baths, mirrors, etc., and every appointment for the convenience and comfort of guests.

NO EXTRA CHARGE FOR STOP-OVER.

Time Schedule of Through Trains is so arranged as to allow passengers ample time to stop off *en route* to experience the novel and exhilarating effect of a bath in

THE GREAT DEAD SEA OF AMERICA,

and then continue their journey and make California connections.

SAN FRANCISCO
TO
Pacific Junction and Omaha,
—VIA—
Central Pacific, Denver & Rio Grande and Burlington & Missouri River Railroads.
No Change of Cars of any class between OGDEN and DENVER.

Mls	STATIONS.	Route.	Atlantic Exp., Daily.	Emigrant. Daily.
....	Lv. Los Angeles......	Cent. Pac. R. R.	7 30 p.m.	7 30 p.m.
0	" San Francisco....	"	3 00 "	3 00 "
5	" Oakland Pier.....	"	3 28 "	3 28 "
90	" Sacramento	"	*7 20 "	*7 20 "
145	" Colfax...........	"	11 20 "	11 20 "
210	" Truckee..........	"	4 50 a.m.	4 50 a.m.
245	" Reno.............	"	*7 00 "	*7 00 "
415	" Winnemucca......	"	1 45 p.m.	1 45 p.m.
475	" Battle Mountain..	"	3 50 "	3 50 "
526	" Palisade.........	"	5 46 "	5 46 "
558	" Elko.............	"	*7 40 "	*7 40 "
742	" Kelton...........	"	3 55 a.m.	3 55 a.m.
809	" Corinne..........	"	6 52 "	6 52 "
833	Ar. Ogden	"	*7 55 "	*7 55 "
0	Lv. Ogden	D.&R.G.W.R'y	9 40 "	9 40 "
36	Ar. Salt Lake	"	11 05 "	11 05 "
36	Lv. Salt Lake	"	11 15 "	11 15 "
47	" Bingham Junction	"	11 39 "	11 39 "
82	Ar. Provo............	"	12 50 p.m.	12 50 p.m.
82	Lv. Provo............	"	1 10 "	1 10 "
87	" Springville.......	"	1 22 "	1 22 "
134	Ar. P. V. Junction...	"	3 50 "	3 50 "
134	Lv. P. V. Junction...	"	3 50 "	3 50 "
227	Ar. Green River.....	"	*7 25 "	*7 25 "
227	Lv. Green River.....	"	7 50 "	7 50 "
347	Ar. Grand Junction..	"	12 30 a.m.	12 30 a.m.
347	Lv. Grand Junction..	D. & R. G. R.R.	12 40 "	12 40 "
396	" Delta	"	2 47 "	2 47 "
418	" Montrose........	"	3 50 "	3 50 "
440	Ar. Cimarron	"	5 20 "	5 20 "
440	Lv. Cimarron	"	5 25 "	5 25 "
481	" Gunnison........	"	*7 45 "	*7 45 "
512	Ar. Sargent	"	8 55 "	8 55 "
512	Lv. Sargent	"	9 00 "	9 00 "
529	" Marshall Pass.....	"	10 25 "	10 25 "
555	Ar. Salida..........	"	12*05 p.m.	12*05 p.m.
555	Lv. Salida..........	"	12 25 "	12 25 "
610	" Canon City......	"	2 43 "	2 43 "
651	Ar. South Pueblo....	"	†4 13 "	†4 13 "
651	Lv. South Pueblo....	"	4 25 "	4 25 "
696	Ar. Colorado Springs.	"	6 03 "	6 03 "
696	Lv. Colorado Springs.	"	6 08 "	6 08 "
719	" Palmer Lake	"	†7 15 "	†7 15 "
771	Ar. Denver..........	"	9 10 "	9 10 "
0	Lv. Denver..........	..B. & M. R.R.	9 55 "	9 55 "
254	Ar. McCook	"	5 35 a.m.	5 35 a.m.
254	Lv. McCook	"	6 40 "	6 40 "
386	Ar. Hastings........	"	11 33 "	11 33 "
386	Lv. Hastings........	"	11 43 "	11 43 "
483	Ar. Lincoln.........	"	3 25 p.m.	3 25 p.m.
483	Lv. Lincoln.........	"	4 00 "	4 00 "
534	Ar. Oreapolis	"	6 15 "	6 15 "
....	Lv. Lincoln	..B. & M. R.R.	3 50 p.m.	3 50 p.m.
....	Ar. Omaha	"	5 30 "	5 30 "
534	Lv. Oreapolis........	..B. & M. R.R.	6 20 p.m.	6 20 p.m.
550	Ar. Omaha	"	6 55 "	6 55 "
534	Lv. Oreapolis........	..B. & M. R.R.	6 15 p.m.	6 15 p.m.
543	Ar. Pacific Junction..	"	6 55 "	6 55 "

By 1887 the separate "Emigrant" train had been eliminated, its schedule now coinciding with that of the "Atlantic" and "Pacific" express. The latter's schedule had been speeded up slightly, and readjusted so that — unfortunately — the Black Canon and Cerro Summit were traversed in darkness both directions. However, the railroad was now actively promoting the new Lake Park beach resort north of Salt Lake City. (Museum Coll.)

But as Malloy braked the train to a stop, six masked men armed with rifles appeared out of the brush and one yelled "Get down out of there" to the engine crew. Malloy had just been paid, and he surreputitiously threw his wallet containing $900 into the coal in the tender, where it remained undiscovered by the outlaws. The conductor sent a brakeman on foot back down the track to Grand Junction, and he got away unobserved by the robbers. Then the conductor and a passenger walked up alongside the train until the outlaws fired over their heads and ordered them to stop. The mail route agent and the baggage agent were ordered to open their respective cars, and the latter at first refused, but was induced by threats to comply. However, he did not know the combination of the safe; express safe combinations were known only by station agents along the route, and the train robbers, not realizing this, had not brought any explosives with them. The outlaws had ordered the passengers to remain in their cars, and did not molest them; consequently all the "Wild Bunch" got away with was the registered mail — 23 letters which may or may not have contained money or money orders. The robbers then removed the track obstruction themselves, ordered the train on its way, and disappeared into trees on the other side of the river. The *Atlantic Express* went on its way to Denver, and the news of the robbery, the first on this line, caused quite a sensation in Colorado and Utah.

A Denver newspaper reported that the robbers had been "very gentlemanly," although one outlaw had threatened to kill the baggage agent and had been restrained by another of the gang. However, the same Denver paper claimed in a headline that "Four Bungling Maskers Make a Very Poor Job of It," and said that the gang was "clearly green at the business." In fact, this robbery established a *modus operandi* for future crimes such as the famous Wilcox robbery on the Union Pacific, except that in the future the "Wild Bunch" would be better prepared, bringing with them dynamite with which to blow express safes.

No one at the time knew who the members of the gang were, and the Grand Junction posse which pursued them failed to catch them. But eventually the Pinkerton National Detective Agency ascertained that the outlaw who had discouraged one of his companions from murdering the baggage agent was one George Leroy Parker, alias "Butch Cassidy." Fortunately for the Rio Grande, the gang went on to bigger things, and did not rob the narrow gauge in Colorado again.

Most trips over the line from Salt Lake to Denver were less exciting than that run in November 1887. In 1889 the British poet and arch-imperialist Rudyard Kipling returned from India to England by way of this narrow gauge line. He had the misfortune to sit with a biscuit salesman who was also a Baptist with missionary urges, and Kipling apparently got a good dose of religion across the deserts of eastern Utah.

"The sun baked the car-roof, and the dust caked the windows," he noted in a letter recounting his experiences, "and through the dust and the glare the man with the biscuits bore witness to his creed . . ."

The heat was stifling. We quitted the desert and launched into the rolling green plains of Colorado. Dozing uneasily with every removable rag removed, I was roused by a blast of intense cold and the drumming of a hundred drums. The train had stopped. Far as the eye could range the land was white under two feet of hail—each hailstone as big as the top of a sherry-glass. I saw a young colt by the side of the track standing with his poor little fluffy back to the pitiless pelting. He was pounded to death. An old horse met his doom on the run. He galloped wildly towards the train, but his hind legs dropped into a hole half water and half ice. He beat the ground with his fore-feet for a minute and then rolling over on his side submitted quietly to be killed.

When the storm ceased, we picked our way cautiously and crippledly over a track that might give way at any moment.

The track didn't spread, but the crew was apparently afraid it would at one point:

We began to climb hills, and then we stopped — at night in darkness, while men threw sand under the wheels and crow-barred the track and then "guessed" that we might proceed. Not being in the least anxious to face my Maker half asleep and rubbing my eyes, I went forward to a common car, and was rewarded by two hours' conversation with the stranded, broken-down husband-abandoned actress of a fourth-rate, stranded, broken-down, manager-bereft company. She was muzzy with beer, reduced to her last dollar, fearful that there would be no one to meet her in Omaha, and wept at intervals because she had given the conductor a five-dollar bill to change and he hadn't come back. He was an Irishman, so I knew he couldn't steal, and I addressed myself to the task of consolation.

Kipling was rewarded with the woman's life story. Eventually the conductor reappeared with the five-dollar bill "honestly changed" and the woman wept again out of a combination of beer and gratitude and soon fell asleep. He decided she was almost beautiful and "quite kissable," but omitted to say whether or not he did. "Yes," he added, "we were a queer company going up to the Rockies together." Somewhere in the vicinity of Montrose they suffered a breakdown and were delayed 12 hours, during which time Kipling ate all of the Baptist's sample-biscuits. "They were various in composition, but nourishing," he concluded: "Always travel with a 'drummer'."

The Englishman was most impressed with the Black Canon of the Gunnison.

We had been climbing for very many hours, and attained a modest elevation of some seven or eight thousand feet above the sea, when we entered a gorge, remote from the sun, where the rocks were two thousand feet sheer, and where a rock-splintered river roared and howled ten feet below a track which seemed to have been built on the simple principle of

89

After the railroad company had recuperated from the expense of initial construction of the line, further construction activities were undertaken in later years for line improvements and for the opening of branches into new territory. At left a work gang holes through a new tunnel with the benefit of what appears to be the most rudimentary equipment. (Utah State Historical Society Coll.) Below, a team hauling a huge bridge timber stops to pose while passing scraper teams working on the grade of the new Eureka Hill-Gemini branch. (Larry M. Southwick Coll.)

dropping miscellaneous dirt into the river and pinning a few rails a-top. There was a glory and a wonder and a mystery about that mad ride which I felt keenly (you will find it properly dressed up in the guide-books), until I had to offer prayers for the safety of the train. There was no hope of seeing the track two hundred yards ahead. We seemed to be running into the bowels of the earth at the invitation of an irresponsible stream. Then the solid rock would open and disclose a curve of awful twistfulness. Then the driver (an English term for engineer) put on all steam, and we would go round that curve on one wheel chiefly, the Gunnison River gnashing its teeth below. The cars overhung the edge of the water, and if a single one of the rails had chosen to spread, nothing in the wide world could have saved us from drowning. I knew we should damage something in the end—the somber horrors of the gorge, the rush of the jade-green water below, and the cheerful tales told by the conductor made me certain of the catastrophe.

There was nothing like a loquacious conductor to calm a nervous passenger's fears!

Kipling also experienced the common occurence of the train hitting some livestock a couple of miles west of Gunnison, where there was a stretch of track with water backed up on both sides.

The locomotive gave one wild "Hoo! Hoo! Hoo!" but it was too late. He was a beautiful bull, and goodness only knows why he had chosen the track for a constitutional with his wife. *She* was flung to the left, but the cow-catcher caught *him* and turning him around, heaved him shoulder deep into the pool. The expression of blank, blind bewilderment on his bovine, jovine face was wonderful to behold. He was not angry. I don't think he was even scared, though he must have flown ten yards through the air. All he wanted to know was: "Will somebody have the goodness to tell a respectable old gentleman what in the world, or out of it, has occurred?"

The train was not derailed and raced on towards town.

If the Black Canon had impressed Kipling, the town of Gunnison did not. Five minutes down the track from where they had hit the bull,

the stream that had been snapping at our heels in the gorges split itself into a dozen silver threads on a breezy upland and became an innocent trout beck, and we halted at a half-dead city, the name of which does not remain with me. It had originally been built on the crest of a wave of prosperity. Once ten thousand people had walked its street; but the boom had collapsed. The great brick houses and the factories were empty. The population lived in little timber shanties on the fringes of the deserted town. There were some railway workshops and things, and the hotel (whose pavement formed the platform of the railway) contained one hundred and more rooms, empty.

A Chicago lawyer joined the party, and though he made an ass of himself by staid British standards, Kipling found his unrestrained enthusiasm refreshing and full of common sense. They talked politics and trout-flies during a day's layover while fishing up and down the shallows of a nearby creek, and Kipling ended the day catching a three-pounder after "ten minutes' excited argument" using a "ragged old brown hackle." He tried to entice a small boy living with his parents and three or four brothers and sisters to show him where fishing along the Gunnison was best, but the boy had done it so much he was bored with the idea and not even six shillings would move him. His maw wouldn't force him, treating him, Kipling recounted, "as though he were one of the elemental forces of nature instead of a spankable brat . . ." The father similarly refused to intervene. The thing that really bothered Kipling was how the woman, once a schoolteacher, had arrived in this "mucky tenement" and why, and how, though preserving her pretty New England accent, she had come to regard washing as a luxury. The whole family was

caked with filth. Even more puzzling, the father, between quids of chewing tobacco, spoke like a well-educated man. "There was a story there," the writer commented regretfully, "but I couldn't get at it."

The next day Kipling boarded the eastbound train and rode over Marshall Pass. "Up to that time," he conceded, "our climbing didn't count." He described the process of "doubling the hill":

The train ran violently up a steep place and was taken to pieces. Five cars were hitched on to two locomotives, and two cars to one locomotive. This seemed to be a kind and thoughtful act, but I was idiot enough to go forward and watch the coupling-on of the two rear cars in which Caesar and his fortunes were to travel. Some one had lost or eaten the regular ordained coupling (the Miller hook device, no doubt) and a man picked up from the tailboard of the engine a single iron link about as thick as a fetter-link watch-chain, and "guessed it would do." Get hauled up a Simla cliff by the hook of a lady's parasol if you wish to appreciate my sentiments when the cars moved uphill and the link drew tight. Miles away and two thousand feet above our heads rose the shoulder of a hill epauletted with the long line of a snow-tunnel. The first section of the cars crawled a quarter of a mile ahead of us, the track snaked and looped behind, and there was a black drop to the left. So we went up and up and up till the thin air grew thinner and the *chunk-chunk-chunk* of the laboring locomotive was answered by the oppressed beating of the exhausted heart. Through the checked light and shade of the snow tunnels (horrible caverns of rude timbering) we ground our way, halting now and again to allow a downtrain to pass. One monster of forty mineral cars slid past, scarce held by four locomotives, their brakes screaming and chortling in chorus; and in the end, after a glimpse at half America spread mapwise leagues below us, we halted at the head of the longest snow tunnel of all, on the crest of the divide, between ten and eleven thousand feet above the level of the sea. The locomotive wished to draw breath, and the passengers to gather the flowers that nodded impertinently through the chinks of the boarding. A lady passenger's nose began to bleed, and other ladies threw themselves down on the seats and gasped with the gasping train, while a wind as keen as a knife-edge rioted down the grimy tunnel.

Then, despatching a pilot-engine to clear the way (the helper engine, running down ahead of the train), we began the downward portion of the journey with every available brake on, and frequent shrieks, till after some hours we reached the level plain . . .

Kipling must have slept through Salida and the Royal Gorge; at least he made no comment about them, and he likewise neglected Denver, for the next place he discussed was Omaha.

The Changing of the Gauge

Through the period of narrow gauge operations over the main line to Salt Lake there was a continuing threat of Burlington construction to Grand Junction, which of course would put a standard gauge line through the mountains in competition with the D&RG-D&RGW narrow gauge. There was little the Rio Grande companies could do in the hard times of the middle eighties to forestall such a move, but the Burlington, too, suffered from the depression and never made the threatened invasion west of Denver.

By the late eighties, however, the Rio Grande was facing just such a threat from another source—James J. Hagerman's Colorado Midland began construction of a standard gauge line from Colorado Springs through Ute Pass and Trout Creek Pass to Leadville, then on over Hagerman Pass to Aspen.

Spurred on by this competition, the D&RG, having emerged from its receivership in 1886 under the new name of Denver & Rio Grande Railroad, extended its own narrow gauge line from the terminus at Rock Creek in Eagle River Canon on through Glenwood Canon and

into Aspen in 1887. To more effectively meet the standard gauge competition, in 1888 the company began partial conversion to standard gauge, initially by laying a third rail over much of the narrow gauge. Then to anticipate the Midland west of Glenwood Springs, a 26.63-mile narrow gauge extension to Rifle Creek was constructed in 1889.

In December that year, the D&RG and the Colorado Midland compromised and agreed to build a joint line from Rifle Creek to Grand Junction, with the Midland granted trackage rights over the D&RG from Glenwood Springs to Rifle. This necessitated the standard gauging of all the Rio Grande line from Canon City to Rifle Creek to meet the competition, from which point the jointly owned *Rio Grande Junction Railway* would build standard gauge on into Grand Junction.

The intention of the Denver & Rio Grande to standard gauge its lines was sufficiently clear in 1887 that General Palmer, who had retained the presidency of the Denver & Rio Grande Western Railway in Utah after it emerged from receivership in 1886, recognized the necessity of standard gauging the Utah lines. Construction necessitated by the changing of the gauge was begun in Utah in the spring of 1889, and on July 1, the Denver & Rio Grande Western Railway was reorganized, refinanced, and renamed the *Rio Grande Western Railway.*

The standard gauging of the Utah lines was carried out much more thoughtfully than on the Colorado lines. The track was not merely widened — it was extensively rebuilt and rerouted. Palmer was especially anxious to improve the Grassy Trail section which had suffered from washouts over the years. Extensive rebuilding of the Soldier Summit crossing resulted in the construction of tunnels and new alignments that never carried narrow gauge traffic. Similarly, between Crevasse, Colorado, and the vicinity of Cisco, Utah, an entirely new standard gauge line was laid through Ruby Canon on the Grand (Colorado) River, thus bypassing the desert badlands for nearly forty miles, and incidentally providing a standard gauge line about seven

miles shorter than the narrow gauge. Of course in a few places where the narrow gauge and standard gauge coincided, third rail had to be temporarily laid, but in other locations, such as between Grand Junction and Crevasse, standard gauge ties were inserted under the narrow gauge, and as the very last act in the changeover, one rail was simply pulled up and relaid to the 4 foot 8½ inch width. Once completed, the standard gauge Rio Grande Western would be a different railroad, and the Colorado line no less so, for through standard gauge traffic to Denver would be routed from Grand Junction through Glenwood Springs and Leadville rather than through Montrose and Gunnison.

Toward the end of its narrow gauge days, the Rio Grande Western was a dangerous company to work for, and railroading on the Utah lines was tough work. "Our burned-out engines were falling to pieces and traffic was far too heavy for a single-track line already congested with work trains," recalled one old railroader who had gone to work for the Western as a telegrapher in the Salt Lake City dispatcher's office in 1890.

The equipment on the line was suffering from age and deferred maintenance: "Our dingy coal-burners with high stacks were shaking to pieces on the road; the creaky black passenger cars which once had glittered with brass were showering the track with nuts and bolts. Our little four-door boxcars — they had narrow end doors and platforms ten inches wide—banged along on flat wheels and our track was like toothpaste out of a tube." Yet the management wanted to spend no money for repairs, since the equipment would be scrapped or sold once the standard gauging was completed. "The men didn't like it," recalled Telegrapher Reynolds: "Almost every day somebody would turn up missing when the callboy went after him; so there was a chronic shortage of experienced conductors, brakemen and enginemen."

One day an old acquaintance of Reynolds off the Northern Pacific showed up seeking a job; but when Reynolds talked of the RGW the NP man, Wells, put on a sour ex-

Standard gauging did not eliminate all traces of the RGW's narrow gauge origins. Some of the equipment was converted also, witness "widened-out" Baldwin 2-8-0 no. 11 (formerly D&RG no. 275) and the slim-gauge coach perched on broad-gauge trucks below. Soldiers Summit (bottom) still featured stub switches when new standard gauge RGW 2-8-0 no. 114 thrust its nose out of the snowshed. (Utah State Historical Society.)

pression and said, "No narrow-gauge job for me, Reynolds. Too many things go bust. I thought you might know of something in standard gauge."

"Standard?" replied Reynolds with a chuckle. "We'll be standard in a few months," and he talked Wells into hiring on as a brakeman.

Wells went out early the following morning. When Reynolds went on duty at 8 a.m. a message came in over the wire advising of another accident on the road, a man crushed while coupling cars. The man was Wells, and he did not even live to reach the hospital. A shaken Reynolds vowed to himself never to talk a reluctant man into taking a dangerous job again.

Congestion got so bad in the spring of 1890 that RGW dispatchers occasionally gave up trying to arrange meets and put out orders for trains to "flag through," which literally meant that a flagman would have to walk ahead of the train for 420 miles. In practice, the engineer ran slow, keeping an unusually keen eye open for a plume of smoke ahead which would signal the approach of an opposing train. The number of wrecks increased and in desperation the telegraph department installed junction boxes at every passing track and put portable telegraph sets in the cabooses, planning to have a telegrapher-trainman on every drag. Telegraphers, however, were in short supply, and Reynolds was sent out on the line. There were never enough telegraphers, but the scheme worked well for those trains that did have telegraphers aboard. "Perhaps the little telegraph set enabled some of us to keep our health when so many others were being maimed in wrecks," Reynolds recalled.

Occasionally Reynolds was called as Superintendent Bancroft's conductor. Bancroft worked as hard as any crewman, sometimes working as brakeman or acting as conductor while Reynolds caught some sleep. Working twenty-four hour days was no fun. When stopped at a siding to allow other trains to pass, Bancroft would get off a barrage of telegrams on company business. Sometimes the superintendent's special train would take along freight cars that were awaiting movement at a remote siding, a most unusual practice.

The freight equipment was still equipped with straight air brakes rather than automatic, and the couplers were link-and-pin, as Reynolds recalled:

Coupling pins and links wore out constantly, and there was always a shortage, but you could find them on the ground unless there was snow. Often they snapped while a train was chopping along; one link or pin would snap and the jostling of the cars would shear off two or three others. Trains would break into three parts going down grade. This was a delicate situation even when there happened to be a brakeman on each part. When no man was riding the wild cars, catching them was like snaring an egg thrown out of a window.

In April, Reynolds was using a box car as a caboose, with the side doors nailed up tight and a coal fire in the stove near the rear door. Working west of the summit at Crevasse, he lay down to catch a nap. A few minutes later he was nearly bounced out of the bunk, for the caboose was hopping like a kangaroo, having jumped the rails on passing a stub switch, without the engineer realizing it. The brakeman unloaded out the rear door, but the stove fell over and started a fire which blocked Reynolds from that exit. There was a door at the front but the car was jack-knifing so that a man who tried jumping there stood a good chance of getting crushed. Reynolds noticed then that only a kingpin secured the drawbar to the weaving caboose, and decided to take the chance. He timed it just right and hit the ground, somersaulting down a low fill. By that time the engineer or fireman had noticed the derailed caboose they were dragging and applied the brakes. Reynolds and the brakeman managed to put out the fire with blankets and the water in the cooler, in the process "cursing all narrow-gage pikes and especially those which couldn't keep themselves in repair."

The month of May was pure hell as standard gauging neared completion. Forty or more work trains cluttered up the Rio Grande Western, and each passenger or freight train had to clear them. Reynolds fell farther and farther behind on his train reports, and a car accountant threatened to fire him if he didn't keep up. But his trainmaster, Guinn, told him to take a rest when necessary and get them done when he could. Narrow gauge freights averaged thirty-five cars and there was a lot of paper work involved. At one point Reynolds was three trips behind in his paperwork. But his parents back in Michigan depended in part on his salary, so he couldn't let up and take a chance on getting fired.

One day as narrow gauge operations neared an end, he worked a double-headed freight that pulled into the curved passing track at Crescent, Utah, to await a three and a half hour late passenger train. The siding held a boxcar, a flat and three coal cars, but Reynolds knew his freight could fit in too, once the cars on the siding were pushed together and coupled. Having completed this maneuver, Reynolds sat down in his caboose, sharpened his pencil and got to work on his papers. A little later, hearing the sound of the passenger train roaring down from Thompson Springs, he stepped outside to watch.

It was long for a narrow gauge train, twelve to fourteen cars usually, including some antique Pullmans. "It was not very picturesque," Reynolds noted, "for any colored striping or brasswork she may have had were all repainted a sooty black."

Reynolds walked along his train to check out the coal cars at the siding as the express pounded over the east switch and thundered down alongside the freight. Reynolds then casually glanced at the west switch, and much to his horror saw that it was opened for the siding—if the passenger train hit that it would be wrecked. He scrambled down the embankment and raced the hundred and fifty feet to the switch, hoping the engineer of the passenger would see him and hit the brakes; but he could hear that the engine behind him had not slackened speed. It was nearly a tie between the conductor and the engine of the "varnish" train; but Reynolds was barely in time, the padlock was fortunately hanging unlocked, and the conductor was able to throw the switch closed just as the pilot wheels approached. The enginemen on the passenger weren't paying attention and never saw him. He wrapped his arms around the switch stand to keep from being pulled under the rushing train by the suction, and after being showered with sand kicked up by the train's passage, watched the marker lights on the rear car disappear in the dusk.

The freight brakeman, Andrews, admitted that he had expected that the freight would be too long for the siding and would have to "saw by" the passenger, that he had therefore opened the switch at the other end of the siding, and forgotten to close it. "Many a fine railroader has known such lapses," commented Reynolds magnanimously—that lapse could have killed most of the passengers on that train. But nothing more was said of the incident. "It was just one of a hundred things that happened the year we changed the gauge," Reynolds remembered.

In June, when the final narrow gauge trains were run, confusion reached a new high. Reynolds was conductor of one of the last slim gauge trains to pull into Grand Junction from the west, delivering to the D&RG all of its cars that had strayed out onto the Rio Grande Western in interchange service. Then the freight crews hurried westward again, taking all RGW narrow gauge equipment out of Grand Junction except some being sold second-hand to the new Rio Grande Southern. Western crews then had to clear out all the sidings, moving westward.

A D&RG employee working in Grand Junction at the time later recalled the night when the Western crews made the final exchange of narrow gauge equipment at Grand Junction. Carl Lathrop was a night hostler there. One evening in June, Master Mechanic Struthers advised him that a large number of narrow gauge engines were due in from Utah with D&RG rolling stock, and

that he was to see to it that the locomotives were all properly and speedily coaled and watered for the return trip westward; they all had to be out of Grand Junction by 6:30 in the morning, for a track gang was going to follow them out, widening the track behind them to the point where the new standard gauge line through Ruby Canon diverged from the narrow gauge line north through the desert.

Lathrop had hardly changed into his overalls when the first narrow gauge train rattled in from the west behind a Baldwin engine. Inexplicably the coal track switch had been torn up that afternoon, so Lathrop and his companions had to handshovel coal from gondolas into the tenders. He recalled that

By this time the parade was really coming into town from the west. There were a couple of "hospital" trains among the gang, strings of chained-together cars, equipment that had been antiquated years ago, four-wheelers, and just about every imaginable form of railroad vehicle.

Lathrop and the others quickly serviced each engine, turned it, and moved it out on the long lead from the roundhouse to the main line. By midnight a long string of engines lay coupled together there, awaiting the return of their crew from "beans" and a few hours rest, to start them back west. "They formed an impressive sight, let me tell you," Lathrop recalled, "a sight rarely witnessed on any railroad."

About that time RGW Engine 31, Superintendent Bancroft's shiny locomotive, rolled up to the roundhouse. Once he had serviced her, Lathrop decided to park her in the Number 1 stall in the roundhouse, as this would be the last narrow gauge engine to leave. Bancroft wanted her left outside, but Lathrop worked for the D&RG not the RGW and ignored the superintendent's wishes. As Lathrop was six feet tall and rather husky, Bancroft did not press the matter.

At 4 a.m. the first string of engines and a flock of RGW narrow gauge cabooses moved out westward for their final trip to Salt Lake City. Two and a half hours later

the second and last string whistled out.

Last of all, Lathrop ran the 31 out of the roundhouse and up to the depot where Bancroft's private car was waiting, and at Bancroft's request he switched in a baggage car ahead of the private car. Shortly thereafter, Bancroft headed out on the last narrow gauge train working west from Grand Junction.

After a brief interval during which no traffic moved over the Western as the few final steps in standard gauging were completed, brakemen threw switches diverting traffic from dual gauge sections to new standard gauge alignments, and virtually a new railroad plant came into existence. At 12:40 p.m. on Wednesday, June 11, 1890, the first standard gauge Rio Grande Western train steamed into Grand Junction —and it again was Superintendent Bancroft's special, pulled this time by standard gauge Engine 51, but with the same business car, rolling now on standard gauge trucks. General Manager Dodge and other RGW officials were with Bancroft. Engineer McKay brought the train to a halt before a cheering crowd at the station, and the booming of cannon punctuated the celebration. Two more trains followed, one of them consisting of 8 or 10 coaches, and the first standard gauge train westward left Grand Junction that afternoon; again, it was Bancroft's special. "The Rio Grande Western narrow gauge is a thing of the past," noted the Grand Junction News.

Meanwhile, the grading and tracklaying crews of the Rio Grande Junction Railway were working their way from Rifle Creek towards Grand Junction. The News of June 7 said, "We are assured on good authority that there will be 'laundry' trains run from here to Glenwood as soon as the Rio Grande Junction road is completed. This will give us all a good chance to take a bath." Glenwood, of course, was noted for its hot springs baths. The sound of a locomotive whistle could be heard in DeBeque on Decoration Day at the end of May, but construction was delayed by work on a bridge over Roan Creek, and in fact tracklaying continued at a snail's pace all summer and fall.

Finally on November 15, 1890, the *News* in Grand Junction was able to comment that "The engine at the front on the Rio Grande Junction road can be seen within two miles of town." The first standard gauge train from the east arrived on Monday, November 17, 1890, and a standard gauge line from Denver to Ogden was at last a reality.

Grand Junction remained a dual gauge railroad town for many years, for the line south to Montrose connecting with Gunnison and Salida continued operation as narrow gauge. Branches were extended from it to Lake City and Ouray, and on the latter line the Rio Grande Southern built from Ridgway south to Durango. But that is another story.

Finally the track from Montrose was widened and the last narrow gauge locomotives departed from Grand Junction. The last narrow gauge remnant of the old main line to Salt Lake, the Marshall Pass line, was torn up for scrap in 1955.

Today the winds howl through empty cuts on Marshall Pass, and the dam builders of the Bureau of Reclamation are drowning the beauties of the upper Black Canon beneath their artificial lakes. Out in Utah, a century after the incorporation of the Denver & Rio Grande Railway, one can stand on a forlorn stretch of rotting, hand-hewn narrow gauge ties and watch in the distance long diesel-powered freights speed past on the "new" line. Even the much publicized Royal Gorge can no longer be viewed from a passenger train, a fact that would no doubt dismay Shadrach Hooper if he were here. The Narrow Gauge Transcontinental is gone; "The Scenic Line of the World" a forgotten slogan. Thus in 1970, a century after General Palmer bravely launched his Baby Railroad, history seems to have come full cycle on the slopes of the Rockies and across the deserts of Utah.

BIBLIOGRAPHY

Source material for this monograph was extensive and varied. Among the most important sources were contemporary newspapers such as the following: Crested Butte Republican; Denver Republican; Deseret News (Salt Lake City); Elk Mountain Bonanza (Gothic); Grand Junction News; Gunnison News; Gunnison Democrat; Gunnison Daily News-Democrat; Gunnison Free Press; Gunnison Review; Gunnison Daily Review Press; Montrose Messenger; Mountain Mail (South Arkansas, renamed Salida); Railroad Gazette (a trade publication).

Extensive use was also made of the Rio Grande Collection in the State Historical Society of Colorado, comprising part of the railroad company files, including grading and bringing estimate books, correspondence pertaining to the railroad war in 1884, and correspondence pertaining to construction and maintenance of the railroad. The Sam Howe Scrapbooks were useful regarding the train robbery of 1887. At the Colorado Railroad Museum Library a file of D&RG Annual Reports was an essential source.

Published works consulted included: George Anderson, Kansas West; Robert G. Athearn, Rebel of the Rockies; Herbert O. Brayer, William Blackmore (Vol. 2); James D. Horan, The Wild Bunch; Rudyard Kipling, American Notes; M. C. Poor, A History of the Denver, South Park & Pacific; Betty Wallace, Gunnison; also her Gunnison Country. Especially useful was Arthur Ridgeway's manuscript, "Denver & Rio Grande; Development of Physical Property in Chronological Narrative," although it does contain some errors. Various articles in Railroad Magazine in the 1930s and 1940s contain valuable reminiscences of the changing of the gauge in 1889-1890, as well as Lewis Lathrop's reminiscences of operations on the Marshall Pass-Black Canon line in the 1880s.

ACKNOWLEDGMENTS

One of an author's pleasures is thanking those who have helped him to research and write a monograph such as this; one of an author's despairs is finding that space will not permit listing everyone by name. For lack of space I must acknowledge the assistance of the institutions involved; I cannot name each person within these institutions who helped. I am indebted to the staff of the newspaper room of the Kansas State Historical Society in Topeka, and the staffs of the State Historical Society of Colorado, the Utah Historical Society in Salt Lake City, Brigham Young University Library in Provo, the Historical Museum and Institute of Western Colorado in Grand Junction, the Mesa County Public Library in Grand Junction, the Denver Public Library, and the Grand Junction Daily Sentinel.

There are a few individuals who for the amount of time they contributed deserve special mention: Susan Niemenen and Terry Mangan of the State Historical Society of Colorado were especially helpful. R. W. Richardson of the Colorado Railroad Museum participated in research in the field and in various libraries, and read the manuscript critically. Larry M. Southwick was responsible for researching and obtaining the outstanding selection of early Utah photographs from the collections of the Church of Jesus Christ of Latter Day Saints and the University of Utah. John Buvinger executed the map of Grand Junction from information supplied by Mike McLaughlin, and James Ozment provided valuable timetable information. Finally, I am indebted to the editor of the Colorado Rail Annual, Cornelius Hauck, for the vast amount of work he has put into this publication, as well as his patience in the face of repeated delays. My thanks to all who helped in any way.

Full Cycle: *Desert Siding, the desolate spot in eastern Utah where the D&RG and Western forces met in the building of the narrow gauge, still sees Rio Grande trains today (Gordon Chappell photo). West of Cisco, however, long stretches of abandoned grade and hand-hewn ties — some still holding 30-lb. rail braces and spikes — trace the route of the one-time narrow gauge transcontinental for today's railfan explorer (Robt. W. Richardson).*

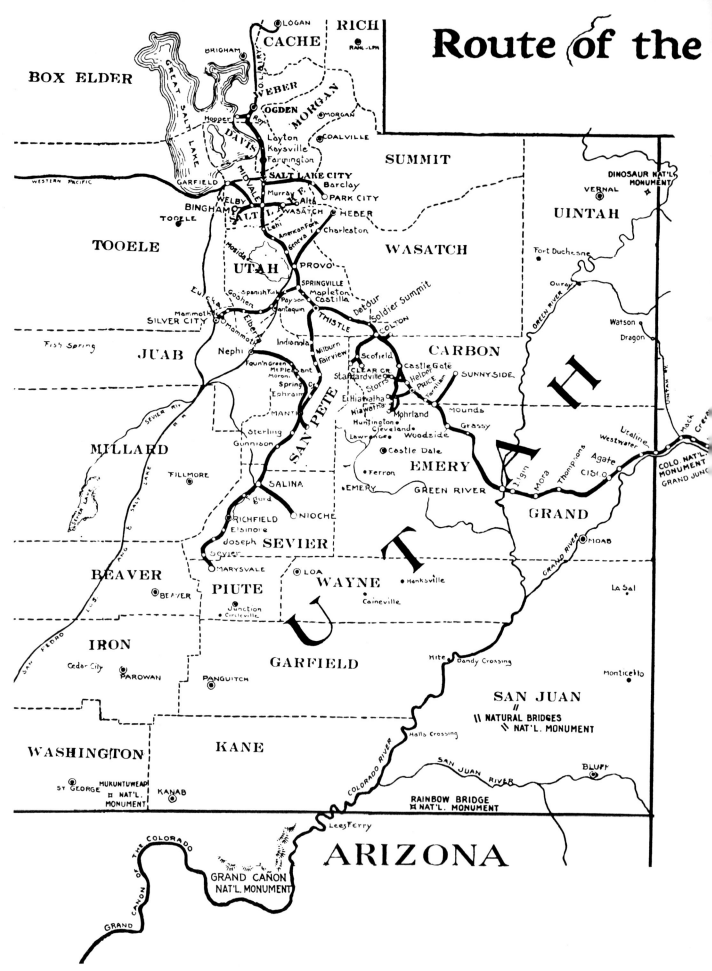

Route of the

Denver & Rio Grande Railroad

THROUGH THE ROCKY MOUNTAINS

Final days of Marshall Pass line passenger service: the Shavano at Salida in the late thirties. Above, standard gauge switch engine no. 1173 dwarfs the little narrow gauge cars as it sets out the consist for the morning train to Gunnison, one July day in 1939; the 479 waiting alongside will couple onto its train when the 1173 is finished. The Monte Christo Hotel in the background is an antiquity from the early days of the line. (Richard B. Jackson.) Below, just a year earlier, the 315 is on the point with the D&RGW's 3-car set of business cars coupled onto the Shavano for the last time. (W. G. Fancher photo, Rail Photo Service.)

Narrow Gauge Transcontinental II:

Black Canon Revisited

Cornelius W. Hauck

After completion of the new D&RG standard gauge line to Grand Junction via Tennessee Pass, and the standard gauging of the Rio Grande Western in Utah, the original Marshall Pass-Black Canon narrow gauge main line was quickly relegated to secondary status. Through traffic now moved via the new standard gauge line; the old line would be forced to subsist on local traffic and products moving from the west slope country to eastern markets.

The loss of transcontinental traffic, however, did not affect the level of business on the narrow gauge as much as might be supposed. For one reason, because of the inefficiencies of narrow gauge operation and the lack of a well-developed interchange traffic with connecting lines, through traffic had not yet developed in any great volume. Much of the traffic on the narrow gauge came from the expanding economy of the

area it served, and the mines of the Gunnison and San Juan regions. The latter, in particular, was enjoying a tremendous boom that provided more and more traffic for the narrow gauge, and this was soon to be augmented further by the building of the Rio Grande Southern into the Telluride, Ophir and Rico mining districts. The area north of Gunnison was already established as an outstanding coal-mining region, and stock raising was also gaining in importance. Thus a swelling stream of coal and agricultural products was added to the ore moving through Gunnison and over Marshall Pass. All this traffic moved over the D&RG narrow gauge; the South Park line to Gunnison over Alpine Pass had been closed down in 1888. Although the line was reopened and operated intermittently over the following two decades, it never presented any significant threat to the D&RG's traffic in the

area, and in fact the South Park's lines in the Gunnison country eventually became D&RG feeders.

The scenic line through the Black Canon of the Gunnison then filled the role of a vital link between the booming San Juan country and the Rio Grande's lines from Gunnison and Salida to Leadville and Pueblo smelters, and to Denver and eastern markets.

The second blow (after the loss of transcontinental traffic) to business on the line came with the crash of silver in 1893. Because silver was one of the most valuable minerals in the complex silver-lead-zinc ores mined in the San Juan districts, the silver panic hit the area hard. But in this case the clouds had a gold, rather than silver lining, for it was then found that these same ores often contained significant and overlooked tellurium compounds rich in gold. Thus the mining economy of the San Juans soon revived; and

Richard B. Jackson was on hand one summer day in 1939 to photograph the Shavano before its demise. Top left, the train pulls away from the Salida depot, crosses the familiar Arkansas River bridge, and heads bravely for Gunnison. Bottom left, the train is already into the steep grades of Marshall Pass as the 479 picks her way along the rocky mountainside. (Both, R. B. Jackson.) Otto Perry, whose photographic coverage of Colorado narrow gauges is legendary, found the train near the same spot (but from another angle) in its last days in 1940 (top right). Thereafter, the line became freight only; and Otto recorded the 489 with one of the last stock extras on Marshall in October 1953 (center; both photos, Otto C. Perry). It was just fifteen years after Jackson had ridden the Shavano through the same snowsheds (bottom, R. B. Jackson).

In July 1936 another well-known railroad photographer, Gerald Best, went from Denver to Grand Junction via the narrow gauge — and suffered hours of delays that almost made him miss his Salt Lake City train connection. Top, the Shavano is in the hole at Mears Junction while the 485 rushes through with a short wrecking train; the passenger then proceeded to Shirley, where it sat for four hours while the 485 and crew rerailed an errant car of coal. Although 4 track miles away, Best could see the derailment high up on the mountainside, and hiked up to watch the rerailing. His wife, meanwhile, caught a handsome trout with borrowed tackle in the nearby stream. At Gunnison they exchanged the 479 for the 319, only to have to wait once again at Sapinero — for a delayed eastbound freight (bottom). Best had travelled the line before, in 1934, and enjoyed on-time performance. The 346 handled the train through the Black Canon on that occasion; at top right it makes a leisurely station stop at Cimarron before tackling Cerro hill (center). At the end of the run at Montrose (bottom right), the 346 posed for this classic view of narrow gauge power at the ready. Sold off a decade later to a lumber road, the little engine was eventually rescued and is now the star performer of the Colorado Railroad Museum collection, and one of the best known narrow gauge engines in the country. (All photos, Gerald M. Best.)

with it, traffic on the Black Canon line. Not only did ore move east, but coal from Gunnison country mines (Baldwin, Crested Butte) moved west to provide fuel for mills and homes. Gunnison, unlike the San Juan mining centers, never regained its status as a hard-rock mining center; but Gunnison coal, some of the best in the Rocky Mountain west, was a major source of traffic to the narrow gauge for over half a century.

Through passenger traffic was, of course, quickly diverted to the new standard gauge line. Local service was still needed, however, and the scenic attractions of the line remained undimmed — in fact, the Curecanti Needle, in the heart of the Canon, was used on the D&RG's herald until the 1920's. A new through passenger schedule was soon evolved that was to remain essentially the same for decades — an overnight train, with Pullman sleepers, was operated from Denver to Salida over the standard gauge, arriving there very early in the morning. The passengers changed into narrow gauge cars in time to leave at 6:30, arriving at Grand Junction at 6:00 PM that evening; another change to standard gauge cars, and they were in Salt Lake City the following morning. Although pre-1890 schedules often found the through narrow gauge express crossing Cerro in the dead of night, the new arrangement permitted seeing the entire narrow gauge route in daylight. Initially the old narrow gauge sleepers were included for the Salida-Grand Junction run to provide first class accommodations, even though it was a daylight run; but soon they were retired in favor of parlor cars.

The first change in this order of events occurred in 1906, when the line from Montrose to Grand Junction was converted to standard gauge. It then became necessary for through passengers to make still another change — at Montrose, to a standard gauge stub-run passenger train to Grand Junction. The parlor cars were diverted from Montrose to the Ouray branch train; for a time another car was run through to Telluride on the Rio Grande Southern. Dining cars never had been provided on the line; in-

The view from Marshall Pass west was spectacular, with the track winding down into the valley below (Shavano tank can just be seen over the baggage car), but after 1940 only an occasional excursion train passenger could enjoy it (top, R. W. Richardson). In its final year, the Shavano was reduced to four cars and patronage confined to a few passengers and a little express and mail out of Gunnison (two Gunnison depot views right, R. B. Jackson). The great La Veta Hotel (bottom), once the spectacular attraction of the whole western slope, had succumbed to a dingy solitude and was to be largely dismantled in 1943 (Richard B. Jackson).

stead, occasional "meal stops" were made at predetermined locations. For many years twenty minutes were allowed at Cimarron for lunch; other stops were made during different periods at Montrose, Gunnison or Sargents.

By the turn of the century, however, the railroad had discounted the Black Canon line as a through-traffic route, and had begun promoting a new plan for tourist business — the "Around the Circle" tours. These sight-seeing trips involved riding the Marshall Pass-Black Canon line to Montrose, then via Rio Grande Southern to Durango (or via the Ouray and Silverton branches, with a "stage" between the two towns), and back to Alamosa and Denver over the Cumbres Pass line. Mesa Verde could be included for those interested in prehistoric indian culture. To better view the beauties of the Black Canon, open-air excursion cars were attached to the rear of the train between Gunnison and Montrose; these were popular summer-time additions and operated well into the 1920's. They permitted tourists to gaze up at the rim of the Canon 2,000 feet over their heads without twisting their necks unduly. Trains would also stop briefly at Curecanti Needle, to let passengers get off, stretch their legs, and view the impressive thousand-foot pinnacle of rock.

Operating practices changed very little through these years. In the 1890's, principal freight power were the 200-series "60" class 2-8-0s; passenger trains were powered generally by tenwheelers. Between Cimarron and Gunnison the line was on a water-level grade, requiring a minimum of power; but both sides of Cerro Summit, from Cimarron to Cedar Creek (10 miles from Montrose), were a steady 4% grade, requiring helpers. For many years a helper engine roundhouse was maintained at Cimarron, but in later years helper engines were sent over from Montrose as needed, and the roundhouse has been long since torn down. The first change in this pattern occurred in 1903, when the new 450-series "mudhen" outside frame compound 2-8-2s arrived from Baldwin. The new 'monsters' were put

to work on the long 4% grades of Marshall Pass, freeing many of the smaller locomotives for use elsewhere in the system. Heavier rail was laid over the line, and after 1903 some of the "70" class 2-8-0s (like the Museum's #346) found their way onto the Black Canon line. Because of light bridges in the Canon — which were never replaced — these "70" class engines remained among the largest that could be used between Gunnison and Cimarron right up to the end of service.

The line did see some new locomotives during World War I, in 1916-17, however. The D&RG purchased six Baldwin 2-8-0s, equivalent to the "70's" in size, from the abandoned Florence & Cripple Creek line—of which the Museum's #318 is an example; and three outside frame 2-8-0s (soon called "little mudhens") from the defunct Crystal River RR. The latter, originally numbered 430-432, were later renumbered 360, 361 and 375. The #375, the largest, eventually spent much time around Durango and on the Silverton line; but the 360 and 361 were extensively used on the Black Canon line, and were the last two engines in use on the Gunnison-Cimarron portion. With the arrival of thirty new, heavy narrow gauge 2-8-2s between 1923 and 1930 most of the "mudhens" were moved from Marshall pass to other assignments; one of these was serving as helper on freights over Cerro Summit. Normal practice would see a 2-8-0 bringing the train over from Gunnison, with a 450 "mudhen" coming over light from Montrose to help the train from Cimarron (or Crystal, a mile east of Cimarron) up "the hill". By this time the passenger trains had grown so short that a tenwheeler or "70" class 2-8-0 could get one over the 4% without help. Because the Baldwin branch was confined to using nothing larger than a "60" class engine, these continued to be seen on the line also; and in fact the #268 was the last engine to run on the line west of Gunnison.

As the years went by, traffic dwindled gradually. Removal of the third rail to Pueblo in 1911 and Leadville in 1925, eliminating through ore shipments to the smelters in narrow gauge cars, paralleled the at-

trition in mining business. The conversion of the Montrose-Grand Junction line to standard gauge in 1906, as noted earlier, siphoned off some through traffic from west of Montrose; the opening of the Dotsero cut-off diverted even more traffic east via the Moffat Tunnel. After 1934 virtually all traffic on the line was local or destined to narrow gauge points. Some stock still moved back and forth through Montrose, and agricultural products; coal moved west from Gunnison in small quantities. A new source of revenue during the twenties and thirties was gasoline and petroleum products; tank cars moved up from Farmington, New Mexico, via the Rio Grande Southern, to Gunnison. Principal traffic to or from points on the line itself between Gunnison and Montrose were seasonal sheep and cattle movements. Sapinero and Iola, east of the Canon itself, were important loading points. Every fall a great roundup was held in the Powderhorn region southwest of Gunnison, and as many as a thousand head of cattle would be loaded at Iola. A small engine would bring the cuts of cars into Gunnison as they were loaded, and assemble them into a train; a 480 or 490 would take the train up the valley to Sargents, where three more of the big 2-8-2s would meet it to help the train over Marshall Pass, and the cattle would be in Salida the same day.

Autos and buses, and the depression, made inroads into the remaining passenger business. The train dwindled to three or four cars west of Gunnison, and the parlor car and R.P.O. route terminated at Montrose. The Rio Grande Southern connection became a motorized "Galloping Goose" and interchange traffic negligible; the Ouray train was downgraded to a mixed in 1934. The end finally came in 1936, and regular passenger service through the Black Canon was abandoned. The Curecanti Needle had long since disappeared from the Rio Grande's herald, replaced by unimaginative slogans for Royal Gorge and Moffat Tunnel. The Gunnison-Salida portion of the run was retained and the cars refurbished, and a bus connection of Rio Grande

Coal and stock kept the Gunnison line busy for many years. Here the 361, a "little mudhen" from the Crystal River, rolls into Gunnison from Cimarron on a fall day in 1946, with 13 cars of stock for Denver (R. W. Richardson). The Gunnison yards saw small power like the aged 278 (right) work side by side with the Rio Grande's heaviest power like the 498, which was too big for the Baldwin branch or the Black Canon line (C. W. Hauck). Gunnison's flat terrain was deceiving; real mountain railroading lay just a few miles away in any direction.

Motorways provided Gunnison-Montrose service and enabled the railroad to retain the vital mail contract. But the respite was only for another four years, and the Salida-Gunnison train was discontinued also in 1940. So ended passenger service that had begun so auspiciously nearly sixty years earlier, over what must be described as one of the most beautiful, varied and spectacular stretches of mountain railroad in the Country.

Almost ended, but not quite. For there were to be a few brief revivals of passenger operation through the Black Canon. The first, and by all odds most unusual, revival occurred in the spring of 1944. The highway bridge was washed out at Sapinero, completely severing all transportation between the Gunnison and Montrose areas. To provide emergency service, the D&RGW instituted a temporary, unnumbered two-car passenger train between Gunnison and Montrose, going west in the morning and east in the afternoon. When the highway bridge was replaced, the train disappeared and bus service resumed.

Then a number of excursions were operated over the line between 1947 and 1949, by the Rocky Mountain Railroad Club of Denver and the Montrose Chamber of Commerce. The railroad insisted on running these from Gunnison to Cimarron and return only, because of a piece of bad track on the west side of Cerro Summit. This stretch, several hundred feet long, was near Cedar Creek, and was laid along the side of a hill that had developed a nasty habit of sliding in wet weather. During the early 1940's freight traffic had declined to the point that trains sometimes ran as infrequently as once a month — except during stock season — and after the war the Rio Grande had eliminated the bother of periodically realigning the errant trackwork by pulling it up after the spring stock rush, and not putting it back down 'til the fall rush.

Finally, in 1948 the railroad applied to abandon the line between Sapinero and Cedar Creek, approximately 28 miles, and permission was granted early in 1949. A "last" freight ran over Cerro on May 28, gathering up cars and transferring

One sunny June day in 1940, John Maxwell rode a freight through the Black Canon and made these scenic photos from the cupola of the caboose. Traffic was still substantial; the consist includes stock cars, oil tankers (Conoco and Texaco), coal and merchandise. The center view is just east of Sapinero; the other two, just west. (J. W. Maxwell photos.)

110

several engines between the Gunnison and Montrose ends of the line. An excursion was run that Sunday, May 29, and the last passenger movement between Gunnison and Cimarron occurred the next day, May 30, with a repeat excursion.

The dismantler intended to start scrapping the line from Cedar Creek east early in June, but heavy rains and high water delayed the unpleasant task. Finally the track dried out and the little #360 started to work with the scrapping train. Rails were up as far as Cimarron by July 8, and by the end of the month the Canon had been cleaned of all rails and ties. The twelve miles of line through the Canon were presented to the two counties (Montrose and Gunnison) to use as a public road, primarily for the benefit of fishermen. Even the line's nine steel bridges were included, being planked over for auto use.

The line from Sapinero to Gunnison, through smaller canyons like Cebolla Canon, as well as pretty open valley and meadow land, was operated for several more years as the Sapinero branch. Some stock in season, and a little fluorspar ore and lumber at Sapinero, were handled into Gunnison by one of the two remaining "60" class engines, #268 or #278; "little mudhens" #360 and #361 were scrapped. The last Powderhorn roundup run from Iola was made by the #268 on October 9, 1953; 2-8-2 #489 pulled 31 cars of stock out of Gunnison that noon. The railroad had petitioned for abandonment of all the Gunnison lines the previous summer; authority was received on December 1, 1953, and the Gunnison depot was officially closed that following January 14. The line lay dormant most of the year. That fall the #268 was refueled, and on October 5 it made a last run to Iola and Sapinero to gather up remaining cars, drag them into Gunnison yards, and make them up into a train for the #480 to take over to Salida.

Dismantling of the Gunnison lines took place in 1955, with the #268 powering the scrapping train over the Sapinero branch during June. Officially retired on July 1, it was dressed up and placed on a lowboy "float" for a July 16 "Cattlemen's Days" parade, after which it was placed on display in Gunnison — where it has remained (off and on, one place or another) ever since. A resort owner at Cebolla had planned to buy a piece of the line that crossed his ranch, and operate it with a pop car; but even this modest preservation scheme fell through and the track was torn up with the rest.

For a brief time, the right of way from Sapinero through the Canon to Cimarron was utilized as a fishermen's road, and it was possible to drive over the old road bed, but this last tenuous connection with the region's railroad past was obliterated by the construction of two huge dams. The first, the Blue Mesa Dam, was constructed near the old site of Sapinero, and the resulting Blue Mesa Lake has covered the Gunnison Valley all the way back to a point between Iola and Gunnison itself. The second, the Morrow Point Dam, was constructed far down in the Canon, near the point where the railroad turned out of the main canon to climb up to Cimarron, and this dam has flooded the entire railroad line through the heart of the Canon. One memento of the narrow gauge remains there: the last bridge, adjacent to the dam, has been preserved and the little #278 (at Montrose for years) put on display on the bridge, complete with a short train. Cimarron has been bulldozed out of existence by the highway department; Sapinero is submerged under the icy waters of Blue Mesa Lake; there is little remaining in Gunnison to indicate it was once the hub of five narrow gauge lines; only the little train-and-bridge monument at the Morrow Point Dam remains a tangible link to the narrow gauge transcontinental's passage through the famed Black Canon of the Gunnison.

The author is particularly indebted to Bob Richardson for much historical data on the Black Canon line; and to all those who contributed photographic material for this article, whose names appear in the text.

The 268 employs wedge plow and flanger to open the line through Sapinero in 1952 (R. W. Richardson).

Denver, Colorado Springs and Pueblo to Gunnison, Montrose and Grand Junction via Marshall Pass

Read down			Read up
No. 15-315 Daily	Miles from Denver	STATIONS NARROW GAUGE June 14, 1917	No. 316-16 Daily
7 30	0.0	lv...Denver Union Depot...ar	7 30
10 20	74.9	lv.....Colorado Springs....ar	4 30
11 30	119.4	ar...Pueblo Union Depot...lv	3 05
12 10	119.4	lv...Pueblo Union Depot...ar	2 45
4 05	215.1	ar..........Salida..........lv	10 55
6 30	215.1	lv..........Salida..........ar	8 45
6 45	220.1	.......Poncha Junction.......	8 30
......	223.9	..............Otto..............	......
7 10	226.0	........Mears Junction........	8 08
f 7 20	228.3	............Shirley............	f 7 59
......	231.9	............Keene............	......
f 7 50	234.0	............Gray's............	f 7 37
......	237.6	............Pocono............	......
8 29	240.7	ar......Marshall Pass.......lv	7 10
8 35	240.7	lv......Marshall Pass......ar	7 05
f 8 50	244.9	............Shawano............	f 6 38
f 9 03	248.5	............Chester............	f 6 18
......	252.8	............Buxton............	......
9 35	257.2	ar..........Sargent..........lv	5 45
9 35	257.2	lv..........Sargent..........ar	5 45
f 9 45	262.0	..............Elko..............	f 5 27
f 9 52	265.5	............Crookton............	f 5 18
f10 00	269.5	............Doyle............	f 5 09
......	270.4	............Bonita............	......
10 16	276.8	............Parlin............	4 52
f10 28	282.2	............Mounds............	f 4 40
10 45	288.6	ar.........Gunnison........lv	4 25
10 50	288.6	lv.........Gunnison........ar	‡ 4 20
f11 02	294.5	............Hierro............	f 4 00
f11 14	299.2	..............Iola..............	f 3 47
f11 16	300.1	............Kezar............	f 3 45
f11 36	307.2	............Cebolla............	f 3 25
11 54	314.1	...........Sapinero...........	3 05
......	315.1	........Lake Junction........	......
f12 14	320.9	..........Curecanti..........	f 2 40
......	327.5	.........Crystal Creek.........	......
‡12 40	329.0	ar........Cimmaron........lv	2 15
1 00	329.0	lv........Cimmaron........ar	1 55
1 35	334.6	........Cerro Summit........	1 35
1 58	341.3	..........Cedar Creek..........	12 55
f 2 10	346.4	............Fairview............	f12 34
2 30	351.5	ar.........Montrose.........lv	12 20
2 45	351.5	lv.........Montrose.........ar	‡12 01
f 3 01	357.4	..........Menoken..........	f11 40
3 14	362.2	............Olathe............	11 26
f 3 27	367.5	............Chipeta............	f11 10
3 45	372.8	..............Delta..............	10 56
f 3 55	377.5	..........Roubideau..........	f10 34
f 4 02	380.2	............Straiter............	f10 26
f 4 13	384.8	...........Escalente...........	f10 14
f 4 28	390.9	..........Dominguez..........	f 9 55
f 4 45	397.7	..........Bridgeport..........	f 9 37
f 4 57	402.9	..........Deer Run..........	f 9 23
f 5 10	407.9	............Kahnah............	f 9 10
f 5 20	411.8	..........Whitewater..........	9 01
5 35	417.3	...........Unaweep...........	f 8 47
6 00	424.2	ar.....Grand Junction.....lv	8 30

Open-top Observation Car Service on Trains 315 and 316 through the Black Cañon of the Gunnison; seat fare 25 cents per capita. Tickets may be secured on trains from Train Auditor or Conductor.

DENVER, COLORADO SPRINGS, PUEBLO AND GRAND JUNCTION VIA MARSHALL PASS

READ DOWN			Miles	Table No. 9 STATIONS		Elevation	READ UP		
		15-315					316-16		
....	....	* 7.30 pm	0.0	Lv.....DENVER.....	Ar	5280	* 8.00 am	....	....
....	....	10.00 pm	74.9	Lv.COLORADO SPRINGS.	Ar	5989	5.20 am	....	....
....	....	11.45 pm	119.4	Lv.....PUEBLO.....	Ar	4668	3.50 am	....	....
....	....	12.45 am	151.9	Lv....FLORENCE...	Lv	5199	2.34 am	....	....
....	....	1.12 am	160.0	Lv....Canon City....	Ar	5344	2.14 am	....	....
....	....	....	164.8	......Royal Gorge......		5494	....	....	....
....	....	‖ 3.15 am	215.1	Ar.....SALIDA.....	Lv	7050	12.10 am	....	....
....	....	* 7.30 am	215.1	Lv.....SALIDA.....	Ar	7050	* 9.00 pm	....	....
....	....	f 8.05 am	226.0	Lv..Mears Junction..	Lv	8431	f 8.25 pm	....	....
....	....	9.05 am	240.7	Ar...Marshall Pass...	Lv	10856	7.30 pm	....	....
		10.00 am	257.2	Lv......Sargent......	Ar	8477	6.28 pm	....	....
		10.29 am	269.5	Ar.......Doyle.......	Lv	8062	5.57 pm	....	....
		10.46 am	276.8	Ar.......Parlin......	Lv	7952	5.42 pm	....	....
		‖11.15 am	288.6	Ar.....Gunnison.....	Lv	7683	5.15 pm	....	....
		11.30 am	288.6	Lv.....Gunnison.....	Ar	7683	‖ 5.00 pm	....	....
		f11.55 am	299.2	Ar........Iola........	Lv	7450	f 4.37 pm	....	....
		f12.15 pm	307.1	Ar......Cebolla......	Lv	7354	f 4.17 pm	....	....
		12.35 pm	314.0	Ar......Sapinero......	Lv	7255	3.58 pm	....	....
....	....	1.20 pm	329.0	Ar.....Cimarron.....	Ar	6905	3.13 pm	....	....
....	....	2.50 pm	351.5	Ar...MONTROSE...	Lv	5811	1.40 pm	....	....
....	....	3.20 pm	351.5	Lv...MONTROSE...	Ar	5811	1.00 pm	....	....
....	....	3.42 pm	362.2	Ar.......Olathe.......	Lv	5365	12.33 pm	....	....
....	....	4.05 pm	372.8	Ar.......Delta.......	Lv	4980	12.10 pm	....	....
....	....	f 5.29 pm	411.8	Ar....Whitewater....	Lv	4665	f10.49 am	....	....
....	....	6.00 pm	424.2	Ar..GRAND JUNCTION..	Lv	4583	10.20 am	....	....

Table 20. DENVER & OGDEN LINE, VIA MARSHALL PASS.

15-Bus	Mls.		*June*, 1944.	Elev.	Bus-16
*7 30 P M	0		lve....+**Denver** ♁ ...arr.	5280	7 15 A M
9 45 P M	74.9		+ .**Colorado Springs** . ♁	5989	5 05 A M
•11 40 P M	119.1		+.......**Pueblo**....... ♁	4668	3 50 A M
....	.....		(*Rio Grande Trailways.*)	.....	....
•3 20 A M	215.1	Narrow Gauge Lines.	lve..+**Salida** ♁ ..arr.	7090	•10 00 P M
f •	220.1	Narrow Gauge Lines.	.**Poncha Junction**.	7480	*f* •
....	226.0	Narrow Gauge Lines.	.**Mears Junction**. ♁	8431	....
....	228.3	Narrow Gauge Lines.	.......Shirley........	8669	....
....	234.0	Narrow Gauge Lines.	........Gray's........	9673	....
....	240.7	Narrow Gauge Lines.	....Marshall Pass.. ♁	10856	....
....	248.5	Narrow Gauge Lines.	.......Chester.......	9412	....
•4 40 A M	257.2	Narrow Gauge Lines.	.......**Sargent**..... ♁	8477	•8 06 P M
....	265.5	Narrow Gauge Lines.	.......Crookton.......	8168	....
....	269.0	Narrow Gauge Lines.	........Doyle...... ♁	8062	....
•5 14 A M	276.8	Narrow Gauge Lines.	........Parlin...... ♁	7952	•8 06 P M
•5 35 A M	288.6	Narrow Gauge Lines.	arr.+**Gunnison** ♁.lve.	7683	•7 45 P M
8 25 A M	288.6	Narrow Gauge Lines.	lve..**Gunnison**...arr.	7683	6 15 P M
See	300.1	Narrow Gauge Lines.	........Kezar........	7434	**See**
Note	307.2	Narrow Gauge Lines.	........Cebolla........	7354	**Note**
9 30 A M	314.0	Narrow Gauge Lines.	.....**Sapinero**..... ♁	7255	5 11 P M
– –	320.9	Narrow Gauge Lines.	......Curecanti......	7075	– –
10 21 A M	329.0	Narrow Gauge Lines.	...... Cimarron .... ♁	6905	4 23 P M
– –	334.6	Narrow Gauge Lines.	....Cerro Summit.. ♁	7968	– –
– –	341.3	Narrow Gauge Lines.	.....Cedar Creek... ♁	6752	– –
11 50 A M	351.5	Narrow Gauge Lines.	+... **Montrose** ... ♁	5811	2 45 P M
•3 07 P M	362.2		+........Olathe .... ♁	5365	•11 31 A M
•3 31 P M	372.8		+........**Delta**........ ♁	4980	•11 13 A M
....	384.8		........Escalante........	4845	....
....	397.7		.........Bridgeport	4755	....
....	408.0		.........Kahnah.........	4683	....
....	411.8		.... Whitewater..... ♁	4665	....
....	417.2		.... Unaweep	4636	....
•4 50 P M	424.2		arr..+**Grand Junction** ♁.lve.	4583	•10 00 A M
*7 00 A M	719.7		arr..+**Salt Lake City**...lve.	4224	10 30 P M
*9 45 A M	756.6		arr.....+**Ogden**.....lve.	4293	*9 00 P M

Table 21—CRESTED BUTTE BRANCH.

Bus.	Bus.	Mls	*June*, 1943.	Bus.	Bus.
‡10 15 A M	■7 15	0	lve. +**Gunnison** ♁ . arr.	■9 50	‡5 05 P M
‡10 50 "	■7 45	10.8	.... Almont	■9 20	‡4 35 "
‡11 10 "	■8 00	16.0	......Jack's Cabin......	■9 05	‡4 15 "
‡11 40 A M	■8 30	27.7	arr.+**Crested Butte** ♁ lve.	■8 35	‡3 45 P M
....	A M	31.9	arr...**Anthracite**..lve.	A M	....

* Daily.
† Daily, except Sunday.

Schedules varied only modestly from 1917 (left) to 1929 (top right). More unusual is the schedule at right, showing the little train that was run from Gunnison to Montrose briefly in 1944 to transport mail, express, and passengers while the bridge on the highway was out (all, Museum Collection).

One fine August day in 1935 Richard B. Jackson found Rio Grande 341 breezing along the Gunnison River with train 315, westbound from Gunnison. Above, the train eases around a curve near Cebolla, while below it passes the Lake City branch bridge just beyond Sapinero and enters the Black Canon. Back in 1930 the train had been met at Sapinero by the Lake City mixed at right — tenwheeler 172 and a combine. (3 photos, R. B. Jackson)

Jackson then followed the 341 after it left Cimarron and started up the 4% grade of Cerro Summit, making these nostalgic photos of the little train on curve, hillside, tangent and bridge. The improved highway that enabled Jackson to pace the train and take these pictures also made it possible for buses and automobiles to spirit away its passengers, and its remaining days would be short. (All photos, Richard B. Jackson.)

Narrow gauge met standard at Montrose. Top, the 318 pulled the Ouray mixed alongside tenwheeler 777 on the Grand Junction passenger in 1940 (R. B. Jackson); ten years earlier (below) Ouray had still been served by a passenger run, powered here by no. 167. A mudhen was added for Cerro, and the train became the Salida passenger (right), meeting its westbound counterpart, with no. 172, at Cedar Creek. (3 photos, Locomotive Photo. Co.) By 1952 the dual-gauge yards looked quiet as no. 318 shuffled about before barking out of town with the Ouray local, now freight only. (Two photos, R. W. Richardson.)

During the last few years of operation of the Black Canon line, a number of excursions were operated between Gunnison and Cimarron (the railroad had already "condemned" the line over Cerro for passenger service). Shown on these pages is a Rocky Mountain Railroad Club excursion in September, 1948. On this page, the train is at famed Curecanti Needle; on the page opposite, crossing the Crystal Creek bridge. The silvery car on the end of the train was the Silver Vista, a steel-and-glass observation car built by the railroad in a momentary impulse of tourist travel promotion. It later burned during winter storage and was not replaced. (Top, Ralph E. Hallock; bottom, R. W. Richardson; opposite, the author.)

118

The Rocky Mountain Railroad Club had a final excursion over the line on Memorial Day 1949, shortly before it was dismantled. Bob Richardson was on the trip and made these memorable photographs. Above, the 361 at Chipeta Falls eastbound, and below, taking water and wyeing the train at Cimarron. On the page opposite, the entire company turns out to witness the 361 smoking across the Crystal Creek bridge for the last time. It marked the end of ⅔ of a century of passenger service through the Canon. (3 photos, R. W. Richardson.)

On a June day in 1939 Dick Kindig recorded this typical sequence of events as freight moved back and forth on the line. On this page, no. 361 comes up out of the Black Canon into Cimarron with a short freight — two cars of coal, a Conoco tank car and a box. Here it drops its loads, turns, and starts back for Gunnison with some mixed freight brought over from Montrose by mudhen no. 454. The 454 then (opposite page) takes the accumulated loads from Gunnison and heads up Cerro Summit and down (bottom) to Montrose. (All photos, R. H. Kindig.)

In September 1948, during the last stock season for the Cerro line, the author caught no. 360 hurrying through Sapinero in the first crisp rays of the morning's sunshine; she had left Gunnison before the crack of dawn with a stock extra for Montrose. By midmorning the 360, with the help of mudhen 454 that had come over from Montrose to meet the train at Cimarron, was hard at work boosting full tonnage up Cerro hill. The crew "decorating" the tops of the stock cars provided an added touch of old-time railroading flavor. (All photos, the author.)

Fittingly enough, the last revenue run over Cerro westbound was on May 27, 1949, to move the final shipment of Crested Butte coal to Montrose. Thus the mining industry, for whose traffic so many mountain narrow gauge lines were built, provided the last traffic for the Cerro Summit line—not gold, silver or other exotic ores, however, but just plain old, dirty coal. The little 361 handled the train alone, bringing the cars up the hill in cuts of 3 or 4 at a time. At the top of Cerro (bottom) the cars were set out while the 361 turned on the wye and dropped back down the 4% to Cimarron for another cut. (3 photos, John W. Maxwell.)

The following day, the last east-bound narrow gauge freight left Montrose behind no. 456 — a long drag consisting largely of empty coal cars. Going through Portal (above) the fireman really had to bale in the coal. The train was undoubtedly broken at Cedar Creek and doubled over the top of Cerro Summit. (Both photos, John W. Maxwell.)

127

In later years stock shipments were a major revenue source for the line. Every October the ranchers in the "Powderhorn" region around Iola shipped out in one trainload to Denver, providing quite a spectacular event. Here the 268 takes water in the near-deserted Gunnison yards for the last Powderhorn run in 1953; below, the 268 brings a dozen cars into Gunnison that same morning. By afternoon, the train has been assembled in Gunnison and sent on its way to Salida.

(Both photos R. W. Richardson.)

The last activity at Cimarron was on a rainy July 7th, 1949, when the 360 and the scrapping train went through town, leaving only a trail of bare ties under the big Cottonwoods — the same Cottonwoods that appear as young saplings in the 1880's photos of Cimarron that are included in the early part of this volume. (Both photos, R. W. Richardson.)

On October 5, 1954, 2-8-0 no. 268 was fired up for a last run to Sapinero to bring any remaining cars back to Gunnison. After poking around the Gunnison yards in the early dawn getting ready, the 268 went over to Sapinero and picked up 17 assorted outfit and box cars. Below, the returning last train passes the famous Sapinero Needles, witnessed only by a few trout fishermen and the "abandoned lines reporter" for a clandestine news sheet. (Both photos, R. W. Richardson.)

Weedy, rusty track created problems, particularly in switching the idle cars at Sapinero, and hand sanding was a necessity (right). But the 268 was equal to the task; in fact, five stock cars were added to the original 17 car consist at Iola. The 268 proceeded to walk the whole assemblage into Gunnison amid much smoke and pyrotechnics, with the aid of two crewmen seated on the pilot beam distributing sand on the rails. Two horseback riders from the Elkhorn Resort joined the familiar fellow with the intestine-shattering carryall in witnessing the event. (Both photos, R. W. Richardson.)

the last link goes:
Marshall Pass

Gradually, various sections of the original narrow gauge transcontinental had succumbed either to abandonment or to conversion to standard gauge, until but one final link with the narrow gauge past remained — the original crossing of the continental divide at Marshall Pass. In twenty miles of twisting, climbing (generally at 4% grade) track from Poncha Springs (west of Salida), the line gained some 3,500 feet in elevation to cross the divide at 10,858 feet — only to drop just as steeply seventeen miles to Sargents, in the gentle Tomichi Valley thirty miles from Gunnison.

After the diversion of through transcontinental traffic to the new standard gauge route over Tennessee Pass far to the north, the Marshall Pass route continued to prosper from local Colorado traffic. The tonnage moving over the line was sufficiently robust that in 1903 the Rio Grande purchased fifteen new locomotives from Baldwin (Nos. 450-464) primarily for use between Salida and Sargents — huge by narrow gauge standards, they were 68 ton outside-frame 2-8-2s, and were not allowed west of Sargents until heavier rail was installed. Originally Vauclain compounds, they were soon converted to simple, and later rebuildings produced many variations. They served the D&RGW for nearly fifty years, covering virtually all parts of the narrow gauge system (including the Rio Grande Southern) except the short Gunnison-Baldwin-Cimarron segments, where only 2-8-0s were permitted. Impressive (in 1905) but not graceful, they were soon called "mudhens" by the railroaders.

There also was talk about converting the Marshall Pass line to standard gauge, and in fact in 1912 the Rio Grande management announced plans to spend two million dollars widening the whole Salida-Montrose route. Numerous other plans and announcements were aired and forgotten, but the most promising scheme almost materialized in 1920. That November Colorado voters were asked to pass on a bond issue to finance new railroad tunnels under James Peak (ie, Moffat Tunnel on the Denver & Salt Lake), Marshall Pass and Cumbres Pass. The latter two, of course, would have resulted in standard gauging into the Gunnison and San Juan country, while the former would have made the Dotsero Cut-off scheme possible and put Denver on a new through transcontinental route. Sectional rivalries and jealousies prevailed — no one outside of Denver wanted to do anything that might aggrandize Denver — and the measure was narrowly defeated. Denver and northwest Colorado, of course, were not powerless and proceeded to build the Moffat Tunnel with their own financing, whereas the people in central and southwest Colorado had no such resources and belatedly discovered that they had outsmarted themselves.

After the nineteen twenties the volume of this traffic began to recede. Mining traffic from the San Juans was always cyclical, and began moving out via the standard gauge from Montrose. Finally, abandonment of the Black Canyon line west of Sapinero in 1949 removed the rail tie to the San Juan country, and the only source of revenue remaining was traffic into and out of the Gunnison country.

Highways had already siphoned off most of the miscellaneous "bed springs and cornflakes" traffic — incoming merchandise traffic and the like — and had brought about the demise of the Salida-Gunnison passenger train. The little train, which made the 73 mile run in four hours, had been extensively renovated in 1937 and was the equivalent of the best standard gauge trains in comfort and appointments; nevertheless, passengers avoided it for their own automobiles or the slightly faster bus, and it was discontinued after November 24, 1940. As early as 1916 the *Automobile Blue Book*, relied upon by motorists for their highway information, advised that the 124 mile route from Salida to Gunnison via Cochetopa Pass (to the south of Marshall Pass) boasted a "good graded road all the way", while the shorter (71 mile) route over Monarch Pass (just to the north of Marshall Pass) was steep and still "rough in places". However, the shorter Monarch Pass route was improved in 1921 and became U.S. Highway 50, thereby establishing it as a major through route. A scheme to construct an entirely new highway over Marshall Pass was launched in 1936, but the plan was dropped and instead the Monarch Pass road was extensively improved in 1938-39 — just in time to write *finis* to the Salida-Gunnison express, the *Shavano*.

The major sources of revenue remaining to the Rio Grande in the Gunnison country, by 1950, were coal, from the Baldwin and Crested Butte branches, and seasonal stock movements from such points as Sapinero, Iola and Parlin. The most important of these was coal, and the largest tonnages came from the big Colorado Fuel & Iron mine at Crested Butte. Business from the latter was irregular, however, as it was dependent upon the steel mills at Pueblo, and strikes and other disruptions frequently led to temporary closing of the mine. The other source of coal traffic was at Castleton, on the old Baldwin Branch inherited from the South Park. This coal was "household coal" — coal used for heating homes and business places — and much of it was shipped out via Mears Junction (11 miles west of Salida) and over the "Valley Line" (that atypical narrow gauge that ran straight down the San Luis Valley without a curve) to Alamosa. This line was abandoned in February, 1951, causing the Castleton mine to close and thus depriving the Baldwin branch of its only traffic.

Reopening of the big Crested Butte mine that summer, after a lengthy shut-down, gave the Marshall Pass line a reprieve; Crested Butte Coal, plus a smattering of lead-zinc and fluorspar ore, provided enough traffic for three-engine freights about twice a week. Before the Valley Line was dismantled, the big 490's — outside frame 2-8-2s that the railroad had remanufactured from standard gauge consolidations — were transferred to the Alamosa-Durango line (where they could handle one more car over Cumbres Pass than the 480 series), and eight of the 480's were brought up to handle trains from Salida to Monarch and to Gunnison and Crested Butte. Two of the antique Baldwin C-16 2-8-0s — nos. 268 and 278 — remained at Gunnison to take care of the Sapinero remnant of the old Black Canyon line and other minor duties.

In June, 1952, the CF&I's "big mine" at Crested Butte was shut down due to a steel strike. Then, on July 23, CF&I dropped a bombshell: they would close the mine permanently and dismantle the facilities. A new, highly mechanized mine that had just been opened near Trinidad rendered the Crested Butte mine obsolete and unneeded. The railroad lost no time: on August 25 the D&RGW formally filed an application with the Interstate Commerce Commission to abandon all narrow gauge lines west of Poncha Junction — to Sapinero, Castleton and Crested Butte, a total of 138 miles of line.

Gunnison was immediately alarmed — there would be a loss of payroll, and taxes: the railroad accounted for 25% of the county's total property tax valuation. Various civic leaders and politicians were heard from, while the railroad dispiritedly went about its business of carting what little traffic was still being offered to it. That "usually reliable source", the *Narrow Gauge News*, faithfully reported the few trips that fall — some stock runs, including one to Wylie on the Baldwin branch (the only run that year) with engine 268 (the 278 had already been presented to the City of Montrose for display); a few trips for lumber loading over at Sapinero; a trip now and then to Crested Butte for ore, with the 483 making a final "clean-up run" to Crested Butte on December 4 for a few loads and a string of surplus empty gons. Thereafter, for the first half of 1953, the railroad ran one trip over the line a month, until business picked up a bit in the summer.

In August the loading of 170,000 tons of slack anthracite coal was begun from the abandoned Smith Hill Mine dumps at Crested Butte, destined for Amarillo, Texas; the *Narrow Gauge News* announced that three trains a week would be required through the fall to move all the traffic. Added to that were the typical seasonal stock shipments, involving a four-engine train from Parlin on September 11 and another from Iola on October 9 — with the 268 bringing the loads into Gunnison, the 489 taking them up to Sargents, and then four 480s teaming up to boost the solid train over Marshall Pass. The last round trip of the year into Gunnison was made on December 17 and 18, and it turned out to be historic if totally unheralded: it was the last revenue trip ever made over the Marshall Pass line.

The D&RGW's abandonment petition had been the subject of a hearing at Salida in May, 1953, before an I.C.C. examiner. Gunnison, in a naive attempt to protect its last bit of railroad tax revenue, failed to lodge a complaint against the proposal; only Salida and a few shippers presented any opposition. It should have come as no surprise when the examiner recommended for abandonment in September, and the I.C.C. formally approved the Rio Grande's application to abandon on December 1, effective within 40 days. The Gunnison station was closed on January 14 and the line was quietly abandoned, officially, on January 15, 1954, with the posting of tariff notices to Rio Grande off-line traffic offices.

Rumors of renewed operation persisted; there was more slack coal to be moved at Crested Butte — but it went out by truck; people from New Jersey, Pennsylvania and Illinois were reliably reported to be "interested" in the line — but no money changed hands (the salvage value had been set in the abandonment proceedings at $662,396). In fact, the line lay dormant until September, when shop men refued the 268, and in October the little engine ventured down the Sapinero line for the last time to gather up set-out cars. After the 268 had gathered all the surplus cars at Gunnison, the

480 came over Marshall Pass and moved them on to Salida.

On April 4, 1955, the D&RGW awarded the dismantling contract to Brinkerhoff Brothers of Rico — who had gained experience in their dismal trade tearing up the fabled Rio Grande Southern — and on May 2 ran a final train over to Sargents to bring in gondolas for the scrapper and take out 28 remaining stock cars needed at Alamosa.

Brinkerhoff started work on May 5, when they took up the first rails in the Gunnison yards. Former Rio Grande Southern Galloping Goose No. 7 was brought over to help in the dismantling, but the bulk of the work was slated to be performed with a steam-powered train of gondolas, fitted out with an overhead winch-powered arrangement for hauling the rails up onto the cars. The Western State College (at Gunnison) football team was recruited for the labor force — good training for wrecking the gridiron opposition that fall — and within a month the Baldwin branch, last narrow gauge remnant of the famous South Park line, was gone. By July 1 the Sapinero line was gone too, and the fire was dropped on little 2-8-0 No. 268 for the last time, the engine being moved as a part of the July 16 "Cattlemen's Days" celebration to a display location in Gunnison's city park. No. 483 started taking up the line from Crested Butte east, leaving Gunnison for the last time on July 24, and reaching Sargents in mid-August. The 483 was turned back to the Rio Grande, and the 489 — which had been handling the loads over Marshall — took over the scrap train. The top of Marshall Pass was reached on September 9, and Poncha by the end of the month. The Marshall Pass line was at last committed to history, the last vestige of the ambitious narrow gauge transcontinental completed so daringly by Palmer over seventy years earlier. The railroad gave the right of way over the Pass to Saguache and Chaffee Counties for an auto road, and structures, ties and stray car bodies were sold off to anyone who made an offer. There was no question about it this time: the railroad was gone.

Marshall Pass
Abandonment
as photographed by
Robert W. Richardson

As time ran out for the Marshall Pass line, Bob Richardson maintained close touch with operations, and spent many long hours following (or riding) trains between Salida and Gunnison with camera in hand. As a result, we have a detailed photographic record of the last trains to run over the line, right down to the abandonment train that literally took up the track behind it and carried it off to the Pueblo scrap mill. Some of these historic photographs are shown in the following portfolio; on these and the next two pages, we see what kept the railroad operating as long as it did: the shipment of stock and coal. At left, a three-engine (nos. 483, 480, and, just ahead of the caboose, 481) train of Crested Butte coal nears the summit of Marshall Pass on September 9, 1951. Below, no. 489 has just arrived at Sargents on October 9, 1953, with the last Powderhorn stock movement. Here three helpers (two visible at far right) will be added to boost the 31 cars and caboose over Marshall Pass in fast time.

In these views, the final Powderhorn stock train has just departed Sargents
— no. 489 is still heading the train, but now nos. 483, 480 and 482 are cut
in back in the train for the 4% grades of Marshall. Above, the whole outfit
is stretched out in the valley in a smoky panorama, while below the train
passes Bob Richardson's camera in a final testimonial to big-time operation
on the Marshall Pass narrow gauge.

137

With abandonment a certainty, idle cars on sidings in the Gunnison area had to be hauled out. On this page, no. 480 was photographed making a couple of turns up from Sargents with a miscellaneous assortment of cars on a nippy October 6, 1954. On May 2, the following spring, nos. 483 and 489 went west (above, opp.) with 4 flats and 30 gondolas for the scrapper, and came back with all the empties they could find, including a long string of stock cars (below, opp.). Bob Richardson rode along with them.

By August, 1955, scrapping was well under way, and the 489 came smoking through Parlin one day with a string of gondolas loaded with scrap rail, bound for Poncha Junction (top, left). Later the 489 was found pottering around the yards at Sargents for one of the last times, taking on coal and water (lower left and at right). Finally, even Sargents was left behind, and late one August afternoon the 489 was found inching along just west of Mill Switch curve with the scrapping train (below).

Scrapping progressed rapidly up the west side of Marshall Pass, and by September 2 the dismantling train was approaching famous Shavano tank, located down the side of the mountain beneath the top of the Pass. The view above was taken from the old wagon road, while the near views at right show the 489 taking water at the tank for the last time, before the train proceeded and the crew removed the rails. Finally (far right) the tank and string of bare ties were left far behind across the gulch as the 489 plodded on towards the summit.

As the train climbed around the spur of the mountain, Shavano tank and the abandoned right-of-way were visible down in the valley below, while the snowsheds at the summit of Marshall Pass could plainly be seen etched against the skyline above (left above). Compare this view with the construction-era scene on page iv in the front of this book. Soon no. 489 was approaching the top of the Pass with its load of scrap rail (left) — and then the main line was gone (above); rail was removed from the snowsheds on the summit, and the last train departed from Marshall Pass on September 9, 1955.

the end

INDEX
to Text Matter Only